THE
BRAZILIAN
TABLE

THE BRAZILIAN TABLE

YARA CASTRO ROBERTS
RICHARD ROBERTS

GIBBS SMITH
TO ENRICH AND INSPIRE HUMANKIND
Salt Lake City | Charleston | Santa Fe | Santa Barbara

First Edition
13 12 11 10 09   5 4 3 2 1

Published by
Gibbs Smith
P.O. Box 667
Layton, Utah 84041

1-800.835.4993 orders
www.gibbs-smith.com

Designed and produced by Debra McQuiston
Printed and bound in China
Gibbs Smith books are printed on either recycled, 100% post-consumer
waste, or FSC-certified papers

Library of Congress Cataloging-in-Publication Data

Roberts, Yara Castro.
  The Brazilian table / Yara Castro Roberts and Richard Roberts. — 1st ed.
    p. cm.
  ISBN-13: 978-1-4236-0315-3
  ISBN-10: 1-4236-0315-X
  1. Cookery, Brazilian. I. Roberts, Richard, 1937– II. Title.
  TX716.B6R62 2009
  641.5981—dc22
                          2008042798

To my parents, Belita and Etienne, who revealed to me how essential the table and its pleasures are.

To my grandchildren, Shane and Maya: may they follow the tradition.

Contents

Foreword

Brazil is a country the size of a continent. From the Amazon rainforest in the north to the Pampas in the south, the scenery sweeps like a cinemascope catalogue of breathtaking beauty. The people are as varied as the scenery: Native Indians, Portuguese, Africans, Japanese, Italians, Germans, Lebanese, and others come together daily to mix and mingle and make Brazil one of the most diverse nations in the world. I love Brazil. And I delighted in Yara Robert's love of her native land the first time we met over a decade ago. We both understood that Brazil's cooking was as amazing as its history.

Brazil's cooking holds no secrets for Yara. In *The Brazilian Table,* she takes the reader on a culinary tour of the country she obviously loves and knows well. From the palm oil–hued dishes created by the enslaved Africans of Salvador da Bahía to the dishes inspired by the Portuguese royal courts passing through the food of the native peoples of the Amazon region, with a gracious nod to the nation's newer immigrants, and a salute to her home state of Minas Gerais, Roberts is an able tour guide. She not only tempts us with mouthwatering dishes, she also gives us a primer on Brazilian culinary history and regales us with anecdotes from her childhood along the way.

The journey is a fascinating one filled with the bright tastes of mangoes, pineapples, and coconut. It intrigues the cook with dishes that put new twists on favorite foods such as Roast Chicken, King-Style, Stuffed with Farofa, and delights with innovations such as Corn Crème Brûlée that could only come from this country of bounty and wonder. It challenges the food historian with its revelation of a culinary culture that is little known to the English-speaking world. Finally, it thrills armchair travelers and culinary omnivores with its brilliant photography, much of it by Yara's husband, Richard Roberts. Whether reading or eating, *The Brazilian Table* offers a satisfying meal that will delight eyes, mind, and palate.

—Jessica B. Harris
Professor, author, and culinary historian
January 2009

Acknowledgments

I would like to thank the following people:

To Richard, for his love, for being the best partner throughout our lives, and for his guidance for this book. To my daughter, Danielle, and her husband, Randall, for their love and for the wonderful family they have created.

To my brother, Marcio, and his wife, Eliza, and my nieces, Thaís and Natascha, and their families for the joyful and delicious meals we have shared together. To my cousins, Roger, Dee, and Helen Roberts for their fondness and support. To Roberto and Joanna Ciruffo, Anne Marie Bruno, Vivian Mester, Cecilia Frigerio, Christine Fox, my hearty thanks, and to all my friends in Brazil, France, Mexico, the United States, and Canada for the fun, the cheering, and vital enthusiasm.

To José Alberto Nemer, and Arlete and Eduardo Andrade in Minas Gerais, for sharing their "Minas" with me. To chef Beto Pimentel in Bahía, whose tour of the restaurant kitchen "Paraiso Tropical" and his garden of tropical delights made my taste buds jump! To chef Teresa Paim, and Aniete Lima and their families for their graciousness and Bahían hospitality. To Laís Castro and family who warmly hosted Richard and me in Belém. To Abelardo Bacelar and Andréa Gonçalves who took us around this amazing city. To Anibal, Desirée and Lorena Lima who made us feel at home in their home in Goiânia. To chef Chris Isaac for unlocking the secrets of the cooking of the Cerrado.

To Martha Cintra Leite in Paraty, an artist and great associate, who creates dazzling table decorations, adding more pleasures to the dinners at the cooking school. To our kitchen assistants, Tatiana Lemos, Márcia Helena Gomes, and Simone Pimenta for their dedication and professional exchanges. To Laurent Suaudeau, Carla Pernambuco, Felipe Bronze, Roberta Shudback, and Dadette Mascarenhas for their inspiring recipes.

To my agent, Sally Brady, for her confidence and enthusiasm. And finally, to Gibbs Smith for offering me a unique opportunity to share Brazil throughout this book, and to the talented team who produced an elegant and attractive book.

Preface

It's eight in the evening, "curtain time." Within a few minutes, eight people will arrive at our house for dinner. Yara and I don't know them nor do they know us—yet. We start with a brief preview of the evening as we serve caipirinhas, batidas, and soft drinks. Then Yara invites those who are interested to move to the kitchen with her and to help with or just watch the preparation of the dinner to come. A few minutes after she begins to show how to make each dish on the menu, many participants decide to don aprons, wash hands, and join in the preparation. After a half hour or so, a sense of play begins to enliven in the participants a desire to learn, and that sets off jokes, cheering, and gentle heckling. It has become fun.

Characteristically, the food she prepares with our guests is all from Brazilian ingredients, with recipes that are traditional, adapted, or wholly created by a Brazilian: Yara Castro Roberts—your chef, writer, and guide through this book. During dinner, she tells the story of food in Brazil from its earliest days to the present.

At the table, the conversation flows freely and ranges wide. Guests who are new to Brazil often question both of us about what it's "really" like to live here, and we answer frankly according to their interests. We love it, and we can identify and communicate what we love about it, namely, its people and its beauty. With Brazilians, conversation quickly becomes one you would have with old friends.

We've entertained people from a variety of backgrounds, interests, and nationalities. There have been vacationing businessmen touring Brazil on motorcycles, backpacking students staying at hostels, a king and queen, nobelauriate authors, artists, professors, chefs, couples with children, grandparents, the young, and the old. After a while, we wondered if there was some commonality in this variety. One day it dawned on us that all our guests had two simple but salient qualities in common. First, each one was curious about the world at large. Second, each had the quality of feeling "comfortable in his or her own skin" (a literal translation from the apt French phrase—*bien dans sa peau*). Now a dinner composed of people who share those two qualities is going to be . . . fun. And they have been. Toward the end of the evening at our Brazilian Table, guests often exchange addresses not just with us but also *with each other*. We call what we do here in Paraty the Academy of Cooking & Other Pleasures, and, by the time they leave, guests understand that we really mean it when we answer, "You are," when we are asked the question, "What are the other pleasures?" Of course, there is also the visual pleasure of the table decoration that is set to fit each region, using only a natural palette of flowers, seeds, fruits, palm fronds, and local arts *and* crafts.

We do all this in four languages when the need arises, since we're both fluent in English, Portuguese, Spanish, and French. When there's more than one language at our table, people tend to settle on some form of English, and the non-English speakers are more comfortable since they know they can retreat with us into their own language (as long as it's not one of hundreds we don't speak!).

The fun that everyone has at our table is based in some part on the fact that it all looks effortless. And it is really, yet it's our own particular set of skills and life experiences that help produce that ease. That life experience includes having lived and worked in four different countries on three continents.

Yara is Brazilian. She was born in Belo Horizonte, the daughter of a mother who directed a catering business and a father who was a newspaper journalist. Her professions have spanned ballet dancing in Brazil, a child development career based on a specialist degree from the Sorbonne and practice in Paris and the United States, and being a chef for the last twenty years with formal training at Boston University. The first article about her in the press occurred many years ago when Nancy Jenkins covered her in *The New York Times*. She went on to do a series of cooking programs for WGBH in Boston that was nominated for an Emmy. Six years ago, we moved back to Brazil and started the school. Again, the press has been generous, and we've been covered in newspapers, magazines, and travel guides in the United States and Europe.

I am an American. I was born in Paris of a French mother, who later directed art galleries in New York, and an American father, who ran engineering companies in the chemical industry in Europe and the United States. I went to the university and graduate school at Princeton and Yale and made a career in business. First, I led divisions of large multinational companies in the United States and in Latin America. Then I opened my own management consulting business and concluded that career by initiating a merger of two multibillion-dollar companies. Now I can and do devote full time to photography.

Each of us grew up in households where dinner was sacred, conversation *was* important, and guests were constant and cherished. So at dinner, we always draw out our guests and never leave anyone silent, since we're likely to find something in common with almost everyone.

We write this from beautiful Paraty— a seventeenth-century colonial village with cobblestone streets, sounds of children playing, no cars in its historic center, and the clip-clop of the horse-drawn carriages that regularly tour the village. In addition, the village is at the center of a twenty-mile-wide circle that contains some of the most varied natural beauty in the world. Behind Paraty is the lush and mountainous Atlantic coast forest (the Mata Atlantica) full of rivers, cool waterfalls, and wildlife. Along the coast are long white-sand beaches lined with fruit trees. Seaward is an array of thirty islands where we can anchor for a dive into emerald-green water, stop for lunch, and swim with the fish between courses. And most important are its residents. They are a friendly and talented group, including families who have lived here for generations, a true sample of Brazil. It's because

of the atmosphere they have created that we bought a house here twenty-four years ago. Six years ago, after rebuilding, we started living in it and we now spend nine months of the year here. We write of Paraty with gratitude, because its beauty and its consequent attraction for a broad range of people is what has enabled us to do what we do and now for Yara to write the book you hold in your hands.

—Richard Roberts

To contact us:
yara@chefbrasil.com
richard@barclayimages.com

Introduction: Brazil at the Table

Whatever happens through the history of a country, regardless of its size, richness, or cultural or political importance, much happens at the table!

Of course there are the wars, alliances, and misalliances; marriages between kings and queens; revolutions; climate changes; the fall and the rise of leaders; and the re-settlement of peoples to be considered.

Sometimes the table may not even look like a table; it might be a mat or a rug under the sky or a shady tree or in a tent. In spite of its mode, the table is the scene where appealing facts that are closely attached to the history of places and peoples are revealed.

And Brazil has not been any different.

It all started in the 1500s with the en-counter between the Portuguese and the natives in coastal Brazil. The fact that the Portuguese didn't bring women with them created an incomparable opportunity for cultural exchanges.

One of those exchanges occurred because the *cunhãs,* the Indian women, were in charge of the cooking for the newly arrived. They cooked in the way they knew best, which was to grill: placing seafood, game, fruits, and vegetables directly on the *moquém,* a wooded platform above the fire that the Indians used for cooking. The food was often wrapped in leaves. The natives and the Portuguese ate together around a large woven mat of palm tree leaves. On it, the familiar Indian dishes were side by side with the new foods the Portuguese either had brought or had cultivated in the new land, all prepared by the hands of the cunhãs and served with large amounts of hot peppers and roasted manioc flour.

By sharing food around this rustic table, a strong cultural assimilation took place that probably helped to craft the fusion of races so important in the formation of Brazilian culture.

The Africans began arriving in Brazil in the mid-sixteenth century. Although they came as slaves, they had belonged to well-organized, developed societies with strong traditions and rich cultures expressed in agricultural methods, the manufacture of attractive cooking utensils, and a great cuisine.

The African women were skillful cooks, knowing how to stew and how to bake to preserve foods. Once living in Brazil, the African slaves looked around, as good cooks and chefs do, identifying ingredients that looked familiar. They also learned from the Indian women how to use the native herbs, fruits, roots, and vegetables. They then added the familiar coconut milk, palm oil, peanuts, and okra to the cooking . . . and soon they had taken over their master's kitchen.

In the master's kitchen, the African woman learned new dishes, but she also slipped in the same ingredients she used in her own slave kitchen, enticing her master and his family's palates. These ingredients then became indispensable to the slave owner's table.

In the kitchen of the *senzala* (the slave headquarters), the African woman cooked dishes with the leftover ingredients from the master's kitchen and enriched them with her favorite fragrant ingredients. Most of these dishes were also cooked for the *orixás* (African gods) as part of the ceremonies of *Candomblé*, the religious rites that have since blossomed in Brazil.

Gathered around their respective tables, masters and slaves came to appreciate the same foods, and their ethnicities began to blend together.

Not long after, news of gold and semiprecious stones being discovered in eastern Brazil spread to settlements and villages along the coast. Tens of thousands of people joined organized groups to find wealth thousands of miles away from their own homes. This movement inland dramatically changed the way the country developed. Primitive hamlets developed along the effluents of the São Francisco River and, to a lesser extent, along the effluents of the Rio Grande. This ensemble of mines and their settlements was named Minas Gerais, or General Mines.

After decades of difficult times in this region, including shortages of food, a prosperous period followed in the mid-1700s. Towns sprouted, and richness and wealth began to pave the road for the Minas Gerais region to become the epicenter of colonial politics.

In wealthy towns such as Ouro Preto and Diamantina, some residents had access to a few ingredients that came from Portugal, such as apricots, prunes, and raisins, and spices such as cinnamon, nutmeg, and cloves. The presence of these ingredients, used only on special occasions, was evidence that such a person had political connections with Portugal.

The table setting was also refined and elegant, with tablecloths embroidered by hand and made with linen and lace. Crystal, silver, and beautiful china were brought from England, India, and Macao.

Dishes such as marinated roasted pork loin, whole suckling pig, baked stuffed quail, chicken stews, and dazzling desserts, all with strong Portuguese influence, became part of the Brazilian table. The African women in charge of the cooking paired with the Portuguese ladies to master the use of sugar to make candied fruits, caramelized desserts, and sumptuous cakes.

These elegant tables with the refined dishes might have set the ideal stage for the exchange of ideas about power and politics, one of those being the first movements for the independence of Brazil.

On a rainy November day in 1808, the Portuguese Prince Regent Dom João VI, with the royal family and thousands of members of his court, hurriedly left Lisbon and boarded ships for Brazil. The motive was Napoleon. Due to the alliance between Portugal and England, Napoleon's invasion of Portugal had become inevitable. When Napoleon's army landed in Lisbon, they found the city poor and near-empty, the treasury and the royalty gone. By evacuating, the prince had guaranteed the throne and avoided the humiliation of being conquered.

What followed next were disagreeable times for the royal family and their courtiers, who found themselves in the tropics suffering from the heat—and everything else!

Rio de Janeiro, their final destination, was a dormant town totally unprepared to welcome such honorable residents. The *Paço Imperial*—the administration center and São Cristovão Palace—became the official residence, and it was not suitable to accommodate the royal family and their entourage. But improvements were made rapidly. Elegant houses and official buildings were constructed, the town streets were cleaned daily, and soon Rio de Janeiro became an attractive town with theaters, public gardens, paved streets, and squares—all with European influence.

With the arrival of the royal family and thousands of nobles, new food ingredients such as almonds, tea, and pistachios began gracing Brazilian tables. While black pepper, wheat flour, olive oil, wine, and spirits had been available earlier, their supply and quality had been very inconsistent. With the arrival of the court this changed, and regular supplies and higher quality of these products were ensured.

Even though most of his food came from Europe, Dom João introduced Brazilian food such as guava to the meals of the palace. Likewise, his son Pedro I developed a preference for the combination of rice and beans. Dom João's favorite dish was roast chicken, which, apparently, he could eat more than once a day. According to the Portuguese historian Ana Roldão, among the many cooks who came with the royal family, Alvarenga was said to be the one the king preferred to make his chicken.

Rio's society became used to the elegant

dinners given by the royal family, where important visitors from Europe were also entertained. The royal cuisine included sauces, decorated dishes, the consumption of breads, salads, complex desserts, and wine—all indicating a strong French influence. Gradually, Brazilian ingredients were incorporated into the dishes, helped along by the African women who participated in the cooking, who threw their zest as well as new ingredients into the royal pots and pans.

The court banquets usually lasted three to four hours, and a strict etiquette code and an intimidating set of restrictive formalities dominated the accompanying ceremonials—procedures unfamiliar to almost everyone living in Brazil.

It didn't take long for the Brazilians and the Portuguese living in colonial Brazil to insinuate their natural exuberance, spontaneous behavior, and informal attitude into the dining experience, gracefully circumventing the usual habits of European royalty and thus redefining the Brazilian royal table.

Immigrants from other countries started to arrive in Brazil at the end of 1808, but the great majority came in the mid-nineteenth century as a consequence of the long-awaited abolition of slavery.

Brazil was then a young republic with a work force that was insufficient for the country's growth. This coincided with a wave of emigration that was sweeping Europe. The Brazilian government attracted German and Italian immigrants to the south by giving away land to families who would work it. Later immigrants worked in the extensive coffee plantations in the state of São Paulo.

With the Germans came dishes of smoked pork and cold cuts, and beer. The German women brought their home recipes for pastries and coffee cakes, which are commonly found today in many bakeries and cafés all over Brazil. Beer, the most popular alcoholic beverage in Brazil, was probably Germany's most important contribution and has become a flourishing industry in the country.

The Italians flooded the country with their down-to-earth culinary techniques from both northern and southern Italy: the fabulous pastas and pizzas, cheeses, and ice creams in their cuisine; the care' of private vegetable and herb gardens; and a *savoir-faire* that is imprinted today in Brazilians' souls! Italians participated directly in the creation of robust food businesses, the early basis for the food industry in Brazil.

In the 1930s, Japanese immigrants arrived in the states of São Paulo and Paraná to work in the coffee plantations. Gradually they turned into small- and mid-size landowners and now dominate the fruit and vegetable industry of the whole country. In recent years they have migrated to urban centers, where they occupy important positions in science and service industries. To picture the city of São Paulo without the Japanese is impossible, not only because of the presence of 1.5 million Japanese and Japanese descendants (the largest Japanese population outside Japan), but because of their participation in all aspects of Brazilian life.

The high quality of fresh produce and flowers found in Brazil today is certainly due to the dedication of the Japanese and their knowledge of farming. Their crops of all kinds have shaped the cooking of the whole country, establishing standards of quality. Japanese food shops in São Paulo are literally on every other corner. They are cheek by jowl with traditional Brazilian food shops, and sushi counters are especially popular in all the major Brazilian cities.

The Lebanese started to immigrate to Brazil at the end of the nineteenth century, escaping from the difficult economic situation in their country. Most went to Rio de Janeiro and São Paulo, and small numbers went to the states of Minas Gerais, Amazonas, and Pará. They initially played an important role in the textile trade and also in the retail clothing business. More recently, the Lebanese have become prominent in the medical world as well as in politics.

Today there are around 7 million Lebanese descendants in Brazil, a higher number than the Lebanese population living in Lebanon. Most of them are Christians, but there is also a large number of Muslim and Jewish Lebanese living harmoniously in Brazil. Arab foods or Arab ingredients can be purchased in almost every town in Brazil.

Brazilians perceive those foods and ingredients as common, rather than exotic, and they are included in their usual cooking.

There are fancy Lebanese restaurants with extensive menus as well as fast-food places that serve Arab finger foods, which Brazilians enjoy as snacks between meals.

Immigrants to Brazil have played an invaluable role in the country's culture and economy, and Brazilians have welcomed them in such a way that the immigrants don't think of themselves as non-Brazilian. The immigrants who have brought their foods and dishes to Brazil have enriched forever the country's already fascinating cuisine.

Arriving in a Brazilian home for a typical Sunday family lunch, one may find a succulent lasagna, a mint-flavored cracked wheat salad named *tabbouleh*, a platter of colorful sushi from a take-out place, and a flaky strudel—all alternating with salads, a roast pork with tutu Minas Gerais-style, the Bahían chicken *xim-xim* with palm-oil farofa, and a stewed fish with *pirão* from the Amazon cuisine. All of these savory dishes are placed on the table at the same time; the presentation is family-style.

There is no right or wrong to the order in which Brazilian food is eaten. Each person makes his or her own selection from the dishes presented—akin to a painter who chooses from a palette of colors. Since there is no defined order or process to the serving or eating of food, it can be said that the people at the table are the ultimate chefs at the Brazilian table!

Brazilian Ingredients

Manioc. The manioc, a plant from the Euphorbiaceous family, once called the Queen of Brazil by historian Luis da Câmara Cascudo, is the backbone of Brazilian cuisine. From north to south, east to west, Brazilians from all social levels use the plant in many ways and in a variety of forms, resulting in a range of fabulous dishes. The love story between Brazilians and manioc is illustrated in the tale told by an Englishman traveling on the Negro River in 1849:

> . . . we found this native who was lost in the forest. He looked undernourished, confused, and covered with blisters; he said he was starving because he didn't eat for ten days since there was no manioc flour! With all the gifts from the forests and the rivers, the native didn't consider them as food: if there was no manioc flour, there was no food (Cascudo 1983).

The manioc is a perennial shrubby plant that can grow up to ten feet (three meters). It has jointed stems and shiny, dark green leaves, and its thick roots grow parallel to the ground, spreading in all directions like a gigantic hand with wide-open fingers. The roots are enlarged by the high concentration of starch and are the principal source of nutrients for the plant.

Manihot esculenta originated in Central and South America maybe five thousand years ago, most probably in Brazil. It likes tropical climates with high levels of humidity, although it may grow wild almost anywhere. It is among the ten most important edible plants, and it is also the starchiest one.

Throughout Brazil, manioc, which is also known as *aipim* and *macaxeira*, grows on small farms. Just like the Amerindians have been doing for hundreds of years, the farmers cut stakes from mature plants, sticking them in the ground on lands that are not suitable to cultivate other crops. Although the plants require sufficient moisture the three first months, they can resist and survive extreme drought, being highly adaptable to soils with low fertility.

Manioc has also proven to be extremely resilient to bugs, insects, and plagues.

The plant matures to its harvest stage between six and twelve months. The crop is still reaped manually, by cutting off the top three-fourths of the plant, pulling up the roots, and then separating the roots from each other. Once harvested, the roots need to be consumed immediately or processed into flour or juice to be properly stored. The fresh roots start to deteriorate within three to four days after harvesting, so, in order to reach the markets, they have to be waxed, packed in plastic bags, or frozen.

The leaves, called *maniva,* are also used in cooking. In Brazil, they are picked at any time during the growth of the plant, and, because the leaves also deteriorate rapidly, they have to be cooked or prepared the same day. Sellers in the local markets in major Amazon region towns finely grind the leaves in a meat grinder and then boil them many times for several hours to remove the toxins present in the plant. The resulting paste (maniva) is then sold to customers. One exceptional dish using maniva is called *maniçoba,* which is made with various cuts of pork and is usually prepared for special celebrations.

The Portuguese, during the time of slavery, took manioc to Africa, first in the form of a flour provision and then to cultivate it. Manioc grew along the coast of West Africa until the 1700s, when it spread to East Africa, Madagascar, India, Ceylon, and Indonesia, where it is known as *cassava.*

Among the hundreds of species known today, there are two main types that are used in cooking. The small, sweet manioc requires a simple process to remove the toxins. It is used in cooking to make soups, purées, dumplings, and stews. The larger, bitter variety is used to make flour or starch and requires a longer process to remove the cyanide. This variety is used to make cakes, breads, and desserts.

The manioc roots are rich in highly digestible carbohydrate (up to 30–35 percent), but are low in protein (1–2 percent) and fat (less than 1 percent). They also have significant amounts of calcium (50 mg/100 g), phosphorous (40 mg/100 g), and vitamin C (25 mg/100 g). Although the root is low in protein, the leaves are a good source of it (23 percent), plus vitamins and minerals.

Manioc and its various products play an important role to people who have wheat allergies and coeliac (celiac) disease. The manioc has become a great resource because of its versatility. It can be used in a variety of dishes; the fresh manioc, for instance, is used to make soups, salads, stews, and side dishes. The starchy flour can substitute for wheat to thicken sauces and to bake cakes, pies, and cookies; the roasted coarse flour makes dishes that resemble Moroccan couscous and is used to stuff vegetables, fowl, fish, and meat.

The tapioca is a great basic ingredient for all kinds of soups and for desserts such as custards, ice cream, and *tapioquinha,* a Brazilian version of the crepe. It was in all fairness that, when traveling in Brazil in the 1600s, Phol called the plant *Manihot utilissima* (the most useful manioc).

By any of its names—mandioca, manioc, yucca, or cassava—the root once called the Queen of Brazil is now on its way to expand its sovereignty to the rest of the world. In fact, today manioc provides about 30 percent of the worldwide supply of roots and tubers and is the basic food for over 800 million people around the globe.

Hearts of Palm

Brazil's Indians used the native palm trees, *juçara* and *açai,* for many purposes long before the Portuguese arrived in the 1600s. Its traditional uses included making houses and structures from the trunk; weaving roof fabric, baskets, and sieves from the leaves; cooking and eating its berries or processing the berries (or nuts) into oil and flour; grinding the roots to make larvicide; and using thinner strips of its wood to make bows, arrows, spears, and fish weirs. However, the consumption of hearts of palm was not common. So one can imagine the surprise of a band of sixteenth-century Portuguese travelers in the costal rain forest of Brazil when they came upon a group of Indians eating a tree. At least that's what it

seemed. The Indians were, in fact, eating the soft insides of a palm tree.

Since then, the consumption of hearts of palm has grown widely because of its delicate taste. It's a taste that hints of artichoke heart, asparagus, and nuts, and yet is completely unique. The original source has been the beautiful juçara and açai palm trees that grow wild in the costal rain forest of Brazil; they can reach a height of fifty feet (about fifteen meters), and their long unitary leaves give a wispy shade as they sway in the wind.

Today, there is a new source of hearts of palm. The discovery of wild trees with promising characteristics and subsequent plant breeding over the last decade have produced a species of palm tree called *pupunha,* with characteristics that make it ideal for growing commercially on dedicated plantations. Thousands of trees can grow on just fifty acres of fertile valley land. They are fuller and shorter than their wild cousins, perhaps reaching only twenty-five feet high (seven and a half meters).

The main characteristic that makes this new species economically and ecologically attractive is that several smaller shoots grow from the base of its trunk. Farmers can cut one or two shoots from each tree every twelve to eighteen months and leave the central trunk untouched, which will continue to grow more shoots over its useful life of ten to twenty years.

Each cutting is about three feet long

(one meter) and two to four inches thick (five to ten centimeters). After the green and hard outer covering is stripped away, the wrapped concentric layers of the heart of the palm are exposed. These layers are, in fact, the future leaves of the tree that will grow out from the shoot as the plant grows. The cutting is slightly conical, and specific uses vary with the thickness of the cross sections.

The only inconvenience in the nature of this food is that it has a short shelf life after harvesting. Refrigerated fresh hearts of palm have a maximum shelf life of two weeks, and in the field under the sun they must be brought to a processing plant within a few hours. Processing, with one exception, consists of preserving cut sections of hearts of palm in brine in glass jars or cans, and steam-heating these containers to complete and ensure preservation for shipping, exporting, and distributing. Brazil exports hearts of palm to the United States and Europe.

The exception is a happy one if you live close enough to the plantations as we do in Paraty, and as do residents of Rio de Janeiro and São Paulo. There we can buy fresh hearts of palm, and that is a true delicacy. The taste of fresh hearts of palm is much more intense than that of preserved. It is reason enough to come to Brazil and taste it yourself.

Meanwhile, the key to distributing the fresh product at long distances is speed and refrigeration. Just as fresh seafood is air-shipped to Japan from the North American Pacific Coast, fresh Brazilian hearts of palm may yet become available in select stores in the United States.

Dendê Palm Oil

Dendê oil or *dendém*, as it is known in Angola, takes us on a trip into history. With its origin on the African continent, the palm oil tree was taken and successfully grown in several other regions in the world due to its easy adaptation to new environments.

Surprisingly, according to historians including Brazilian Camara Cascudo, in some African regions dendê appears to have been used as a body oil. When applied externally, it enhances the body with flattering reflective highlights during dance performances and also appears to correct discoloration of darker skin.

In some areas of Africa, palm oil had an esthetic use; in others, it was used in cooking. It was in this latter capacity that it came to Brazil around 1759, becoming one of the most important ingredients of Brazilian cuisine.

For decades the commerce of palm oil was parallel to the slave trade, and it was shipped to Brazil in large amounts. Apparently during 1798, as many as 1,050 gallons (4,000 liters) of the oil were brought to Brazil from Angola and the island of São Tomé in order to fulfill the needs of the vast number of Africans living in Brazil. But it didn't take long for *Palma spinosa* to be planted in Brazil, and, according to Portuguese historical documents, by 1802 the tree was totally acclimatized in this land, becoming a permanent element of the local landscape.

Nevertheless, it was in Salvador and its surroundings—with its dense demographic concentration of African slaves—where the largest plantations of palm oil grew to be indispensable to Bahían cuisine and the rites of Candomblé. Since the African slave women were in charge of most of the cooking, they skillfully succeeded in incorporating dendê into the cuisine of their masters. Thus, dendê became a permanent ingredient in Brazilian cuisine, and it is used to cook dishes made with fish, seafood, and poultry such as the *vatapá*, *Bobó*, and *xim-xim*.

The palm oil tree is imposing, sometimes reaching fifty feet (fifteen meters) high. It has long leaves measuring three feet (one meter), whose bases are covered with thorns. The palm oil tree plantation is beautiful. When the trees are lined up in rows, they create a shady corridor, and, when the wind blows, the leaves undulate in a gracious dance with the sound of splashing waves.

The light yellow flowers grow in large bunches underneath the top leaves of the tree, and it's from them that the stunning fruits blossom. Black in the beginning, the fruit turns into a vibrant reddish orange, indicating that the fruit is ripe.

The palm oil is extracted from selected ripe nuts by pressure, either industrially, with machines producing the oil on a large scale, or by an artisanal method, which results in a much smaller production. Regardless of the method used, the fruit has to be sifted through a large strainer, and then the nuts are boiled slowly to cook the hard center.

In the artisanal method, the pressure is applied by pressing the nuts under a large stone wheel turned by animals or by crushing the nuts in a mill turned by an electric engine. Immediately after being pressed, the nuts are washed in a large sink, where they release their oil.

After a bit more processing, the oil is bottled and sold in markets throughout Brazil. There are several of these artisanal palm oil producers on the "dendê route" between the towns of Ilhéus and Salvador. During the months of January through February, when the oil production is at its peak, the aroma of dendê fills the air, and hundreds of bottles of this delicious ingredient are displayed on the roadsides, where they glow under the hot Bahían sun.

All of the palm-oil history comes together by six o'clock in the afternoon on the streets of Salvador: groups of women all dressed in their typical Bahíana outfits fry *acarajés* in pure dendê oil. When all the stoves are lit and the dendê oil is hot, one feels inebriated by the aroma released from all of the frying pans. People from all walks of life line up to enjoy an acarajé prepared by their favorite Bahíana!

Dendê oil is the most-used oil in Brazil after soybean oil. It is rich in vitamin A (fourteen times more than carrots), but it loses this property when it is used to cook at high temperatures.

Its composition also includes the vitamin B complex and the antioxidant vitamin C. Although it has no cholesterol, it is very rich in calories with a saturated fat content that doesn't act against LDL, the "good cholesterol."

The palm tree plant has an atypical characteristic: nothing from the plant goes to waste. An orange-colored dendê oil is extracted from the pulp of the nut and is used to cook traditional African dishes. The same oil, when refined, becomes clear and odorless and is appropriate to use in salads and in the food industry. Another clear oil is extracted from the seed found in the nut and is used to produce margarine and oil. The outside skin of the nut is utilized to produce asphalt and fertilizer, and, finally, the fiber left after all of the previous processing is used to fire furnaces for machine boilers.

Cachaça

Assis Valente, one of Brazil's best and most popular composers, wrote a song describing a young Brazilian man who goes out early in the morning wearing a shirt with bright stripes and holding a tambourine in his hand. He swings his body as he walks down the street. He stops in the local bar and, instead of having his regular morning repast of toasted bread, butter, and tea, he asks for a straight shot of cachaça!

One of the most popular Carnival songs describes how cachaça is indispensable to life: a person may lack everything, from bread to rice and beans to even money and love . . . but no way one can survive without cachaça.

Cachaça is not only the national drink in Brazil, but it is also a concept and an entity. Brazilians make reference to it as if it has a magic charm and power to which one must bow and eventually surrender. Cachaça is essential to Candomblé rites, and there are some people who say that it attains one's soul. The word itself has become part of the vernacular and Brazilian popular culture. When someone enjoys an activity or an avocation or shows an infatuation with someone, we say in Brazil that "(it) has become his or her cachaça." It signifies a sort of surrender dependency.

Cachaça—called *aguardente*, *pinga*, or *paraty* in different regions of the country—is the product of the distillation of fermented sugarcane juice, with an alcohol strength between 38 and 48 percent by volume. It is the most popular alcoholic beverage in Brazil, and legally the term "cachaça" is reserved for the sole use of product made in Brazil—the same way that the French reserve "champagne."

Historically, cachaça is directly linked to the introduction of sugarcane and the production of sugar in Brazil during the mid-1500s. The slaves who were working at the sugar mills discovered that the *garapa,* the cooked sugarcane juice that was left standing, would ferment, turning into an alcoholic beverage. Apparently in the beginning, the beverage was given only to slaves at the end of their workday, but soon it became a popular drink consumed by all types of people. With the increase of demand, cachaça distilleries proliferated, and cachaça turned into the favorite alcoholic drink of the whole colony, becoming a threat to *bagaceira,* a Portuguese brandy made with grapes.

In Minas Gerais during the gold rush, for example, the consumption of cachaça was such that a royal court order of 1743 prohibited the distilleries in all Minas Gerais, probably starting cachaça's first steps on its long social underground history. (Only in the 1990s did cachaça exit this social stigma to gain status and national and then international recognition.)

With the excuse of producing sugar, people continued to secretly produce cachaça, which prompted the court to attach high taxation on the Brazilian beverage.

Later, during the first movements for independence, cachaça was converted to a political statement when Brazilians served it instead of Porto wine during important receptions.

Today there are two ways of making cachaça in Brazil: artisanal and industrial. The two differ markedly, in terms of manufacturing process and quality. Artisanal cachaças are produced and sold under four thousand brands by over thirty thousand small distilleries spread across the country. Each artisanal producer makes between two and eight thousand gallons (7,600 to 30,300 liters) per year, and it's among these producers that one normally finds the better cachaças. Artisanal cachaça accounts for less than 10 percent of the total Brazilian cachaça production of 360 million gallons (1.4 billion liters) per year.

To make a good-quality artisanal cachaça and to avoid the deterioration of its juice, the sugarcane has to be used within twenty-four to thirty-six hours after being cut. To extract the juice, the stems are washed and then pressed through large metal rollers to separate the juice from the bagasse. The juice is then filtered and fermented. Sometimes a leavening such as *fubá* (cornmeal) is used; rice bran as a flavor enhancer is

Cachaça (left) is Brazil's national distilled spirit.

Urucum (right) is a natural food coloring, sometimes used as body paint among Amazon tribes.

also sometimes added before fermentation. The fermentation lasts between one to three days, and then the liquid is distilled, cooled, and filtered again.

uring the distillation process, the first liquids to appear, called the "head," carry the most volatile by-products and this part is often discarded. As the distillation continues, the second part, called the "heart," is collected. The heart comprises the quality cachaça that is bottled and/or aged. The third part to come from the distillation is called the "tail," which comprises the least volatile part and is usually discarded.

The aging of the cachaça gives the final touch to the drink. The most appropriate material in which to store the aging cachaça is wood because wood enhances the oxidation that occurs between the interior and the exterior. The most used woods are European oak, European cedar, and the Brazilian woods *umburana, freijó,* and *jequitibá.* The ideal aging time is eighteen months, although a few very special cachaça are aged for ten or more years. The quality of the wood barrels and the aging process finish the cachaça, promoting a smoother taste, a distinct aroma, and a range of colors going from clear white to golden yellow. Each artisan cachaça has its producer's unique and unmistakable characteristics, just like an art piece.

The other kind of cachaça production is industrial. Here, the sugarcane is pressed multiple times and is sometimes steam-treated to remove the last of its sugar content. Chemical catalysts are usually added to the fermentation step to improve the yield of alcohol from the sugar and to reduce the fermentation time to an hour or so. The distillation step is continuous rather than batch, using tall distillation columns that receive the fermented liquid from a series of fermenters. The column separates the high- and low-vapor pressure products and is used for subsequent chemical extraction of the remaining alcohol. Given the method, industrially produced cachaça is much more economical than artisanal, and, while it can be quite good, it generally doesn't reach the higher-quality levels of the artisanal cachaça.

There are two ways of drinking cachaça. One is to drink it as a cocktail mixed with fruit and ice; the other is to drink it without embellishment.

The best-known cocktail with cachaça is the *caipirinha,* the national drink made with crushed limes, ice, and sugar. Although there are many versions with other fruits—pineapple, mango, kiwi, cashew fruit, or star fruit—the classic caipirinha is made with limes.

In a way, caipirinha has liberated the

cachaça from its social underground status by taking it to the Brazilian "salons," the fancy bars and restaurants. From there it has gone to the world; caipirinha today has become one of the most popular drinks found in bars and restaurants all over the world.

The other cocktail is the *batida*, also made with all kinds of fresh tropical fruits or their frozen pulp, sugar, and lots of ice, all mixed in a blender and served super cold. In both cases the appropriate cachaça is a nonaged one.

The traditional way to drink cachaça is in its pure form. Cachaça served pure must be from a reputable distillery that uses a high-quality aging process. It is traditionally served in small 2-ounce (50 milliliter) clear glasses. To really taste and appreciate the drink, one takes a sip and lets the liquid linger in the mouth for a couple of minutes . . . then lets the cachaça slide around the tongue . . . and slowly swallows it, feeling the aroma and savoring the aftertaste. Cachaça served with a meal harmonizes surprisingly well with some dishes and ingredients. Storing it in the freezer and serving it cold gives it a pleasant liqueur-like texture.

The increase of the consumption together with the popularity of the Brazilian alcohol prompted the government to impose regulatory measures in order to protect the industry. As a result, President Fernando Henrique Cardoso (in office 1995–2003) signed a law in February 2001 establishing the word "cachaça" as the name to be used exclusively for sugarcane alcohol made in Brazil. This act was finalized by another law in June 2006 signed by President Luis Inácio da Silva (in office 2003–2011), which contains better specifications on the cachaça and the caipirinha drink.

It appears that the rest of the world is getting ready to join Brazilians in singing the eulogy to the cachaça and claiming how irresistible it is.

Pequi

On a sunny morning sometime during the month of January, a certain perfume floats in the air and a fluster happens in the Cerrado: bees come flying from many directions; birds of all kinds and sizes approach, singing with passion; and the mammals of the Cerrado (coatis, armadillos, and deer) unexpectedly come out from their habitats. Next, people begin to assemble in groups as whole families get together with their friends for the expected great day: the picking of the *pequi*.

The pequi (sometime spelled as piqui) is a native fruit of the Cerrado and was in use by the local Indians when the early Portuguese and *bandeirantes* (Brazilian explorers) arrived. It is a round fruit the size of a small orange with a bright yellow color like a rich egg yolk.

What characterizes the pequi is the strength of its distinctive aroma and taste. Both are so powerful that pequi produces equally strong reactions for consumers. Some love pequi and find it a delicacy; others simply cannot stand it.

The *pequizeiro,* or pequi tree, is the symbol of the Cerrado. It may reach thirty or more feet (ten plus meters), presenting a unique canopy easily recognized from far away. The trunk and the branches are twisted and covered by a thick bark of an ashy grey color. The eight-inch (twenty centimeter) leaves grow three to a stem, are hard with irregular ends, and are covered by a shiny down.

The pequizeiro, which is a pleasure to view at any time, becomes magnificent when it blossoms during the months of September through December. The flowers are spectacular. A mix of five pink and light yellow independent petals—about three inches (eight centimeters) in diameter—surrounds pistils that burst brilliantly from the center like fireworks in a night sky.

Around October the flower turns into fruit. By February the picking of the mature fruit is at a peak, and pequi floods the markets of Goiás and Minas Gerais. Vendors improvise stalls, pile the yellow core in a pyramid shape, and sell the pequi by measuring it out in one-liter tin cans. Or they take the whole pequi from a basket, open it with a large knife, and freshly deliver the fruit to pequi experts.

On those days, in some cities hundreds of miles away from the distant Cerrado, the strong aroma of this exotic fruit is noticeable.

The pequi tree grows almost anywhere in the Cerrado, but, according to inhabitants, the trees that are isolated seem to produce more fruit. There is a popular saying that the pequi tree prefers loneliness rather than to be close to other trees.

The pequi is deeply rooted in the region's popular culture. The Indian tribes from the Xingu River region say that the hummingbirds and caimans are the true owners of the pequi.

For the people living in the Cerrado, the pequi does not belong to anyone because it belongs to all. Everyone has the right to pick it, whether it grows in public or private land, fenced or unfenced—in fact, that's the reason people say it should never be fenced. The pequi is as special as truffles in France and Italy; it is part of the environment, and, recently, people are seeing the commercial value of preserving and increasing the production of the fruit.

The traditional dishes made with pequi are the centerpieces of cooking in the Cerrado, and they are found at all tables, regardless of the person's social status. Besides its gastronomic and cultural values, the fruit also has links to popular medicine. The pit, when processed, is considered to be an aphrodisiac, and it is also used to treat asthma, bronchitis, and colds.

Today the industry of the pequi has changed a great deal, from the farming of the plant to the manufacturing of a variety of products made with its fruit, converting the pequi into the "new gold of the Cerrado."

The products made with pequi include oil extracted from its pit and used in small amounts to sauté foods, to perfume savory and sweet sauces, and to season meats. The cream of pequi has a more delicate taste and is added to stews and cakes. It is often sold in small glass jars. The liqueur of pequi is appropriate for flambéing and is used to enrich fruit salad and desserts. The yellow flesh of the fruit is preserved in fine brine and is stored and sold in tall glass jars. It is used in more substantial dishes that ask for the texture of the fruit and a stronger taste. Next to fresh pequi, the freshest form of pequi to buy is frozen pulp, which is used in savory dishes, sweets, and a delicious ice cream.

Among the pequi lovers and defenders is Clovis José de Almeida, whose company works with the fruits of the Cerrado, including pequi. His company ships the product to the largest supermarkets and gourmet stores in Brazil, and it is now in the process of selling to the markets of Italy, Germany, and Japan.

By increasing the demand for the product, Clovis and several other company owners are convincing people in the region to farm this majestic plant in an environmentally friendly way to preserve this amazing product of the Brazilian savannah. People are encouraged to either preserve the pequi trees they already have on their land and/or give away seedlings to plant more, thus increasing the number of pequi trees.

The Cooking
of the Amazon

Jean de Lèry, a Frenchman traveling in Brazil in 1557, appeared perplexed with the pungency of nature and the many curious species of Brazilian flora. He wrote about how much he was intrigued by the new world he was discovering. Nothing seemed to have escaped his accurate observation.

He saw, for instance, that natives harvested edible berries from the açai palm tree. Today harvesting is still done with a climb.

The Magic Root

De Lery also wrote about an unusual plant the Brazilian natives cultivated: "This plant has a soft stem and it looks fragile like a hemp plant. The most admirable thing about this plant is the fact that the Indians break a piece of it, dig a hole in the ground, and carelessly plant it: three months later this plant has grown impressive thick roots" (Cascudo 1983). Other travelers such as Hans Staden and Gabriel Soares de Souza mentioned a tuber that they named a "yam," due to its appearance, that they saw the Indians eat. In fact, if they had asked the Indians about the tuber that was indispensable to their diet,

they would have been told it was manioc.

All chroniclers of the times exhaustively wrote, described, narrated, and registered miniscule details about the preparation of the countless flours, porridges, broths, and cakes, all made from this tuber that Pohl had classified in the superlative as *manihot utilissima*.

If the cultivation of manioc was unchallenging and fast, the process of manufacturing the various products demanded time, patience, and organization. It was the process, not the cultivation, that had determined the sedentary life the Brazilian Indians had adopted.

Manioc had been vital to the diet of the Brazilian native and had been the axis around which Indian life turned for over five thousand years. Given its centrality, it also became a subject of myth and legend.

There are many legends told about the manioc. The one I preferred to hear when I was growing up is the same I choose to tell today to my grandchildren and grandnephews for its magical simplicity.

Açai (left) grows on a particular kind of palm tree and is gaining devotees in the United States and Europe.

A long time ago, in the middle of the Amazon forest there was a tribe living in a community of *ocas* (tall huts), which formed a *taba* (Indian village). One day the *tuixau*, the chief of the *taba*, learned that his daughter was pregnant, although she didn't have a husband. Her father became very angry and demanded that the gods somehow punish his daughter.

Nine months later the young Indian gave birth to a beautiful girl, who, to the surprise of the whole taba, had very white skin and began to talk and walk immediately after birth. The baby girl was named Mani, which means "white" in the Tupi language. Mani's birth made the whole tribe happy, and that year there were no wars, and there was an abundance of food.

Then when Mani was only one year old, she suddenly died! She wasn't ill and no accident had happened; she just closed her eyes and never opened them again.

The whole tribe became sad and unhappy, wars erupted again, and the fish and game disappeared.

Mani was buried inside the same oca where she had lived. Everyday, following the tribe tradition, her mother went to tend Mani's tomb.

After some time had passed, something extraordinary happened: a plant no one had seen before started to grow on Mani's tomb! Everybody was amazed to see the plant growing and growing and growing . . .

The whole tribe was quite disturbed and decided to consult with their *pajé* (shaman). After the meeting was over, the pajé ordered that Mani's body be removed from that site and buried somewhere else.

Everybody gathered around the tomb. The elder Indians opened it and found to their surprise that Mani's body was not inside! Rather, as they dug, in the place of Mani's body they encountered thick roots. The roots were large with a coarse, dark skin that contrasted with the inside, which was impeccably white.

They decided to boil the root, and, as they tasted it, they concluded that such a sweet and delicious root was a gift from the god Tupã! Mani's roots were then grown to feed the Indians and avoid a year of famine.

The Indians called the root Mani-oca, or Mani's plant, because the plant grew from Mani's tomb.

This narrative of the way this extraordinary plant develops closely reflects the way the daily life of a group of Indians unfolds, how they use their time, and how tasks are distributed among the residents living in the taba.

The method Indians use today to process manioc is much the same as it was centuries before, and its many products are still used for the same kind of cooking. It is common to find charming and rustic *casas de farinha* in communities around the region, where people bring their own manioc and, by using the traditional process inherited from the Indians, make the various products from this generous tuber.

The commercial processing involves the same steps but uses different (and, of course, bigger) equipment for each step. In particular, the step of separating the liquid content of the manioc is done by large presses that bear down on the manioc chips, leaving them almost dry, before they are moved into the gas-fired toasting pans.

The manioc plant grows year round and has proven to be extremely resilient against disease and insects. The plant has a thin, leafy stalk and grows five or six feet (1.5 to 1.8 meters) high. The root of the plant is the manioc itself, and it grows horizontally under only a few inches of topsoil. One has only to pull the plant out of the soil by its stalk to reveal and harvest the manioc.

As in olden times, today the whole tribe is involved, in some capacity, with manioc cultivation and production.

The male decides where to plant. He prepares gardens of manioc by cleaning the undergrowth, cutting the trees, and burning the dried wood. The women bring the stalks they took from a previous garden and plant them in the ground, leaving about two feet (.6 meters) of space between each.

Less than a year later, the manioc from these plants is ready to be harvested. That's the moment when the tribe gets organized and begins gathering everything necessary to process the manioc. The tribe will stop working only when they have processed all of it.

The women are in charge of the harvesting and, working together, they dig out the roots, peel them, and wash the peeled maniocs in the river.

After that, they take the manioc to the house to be grated. There, young women join the group sitting on the floor, and all grate the roots, using large grating boards made from shells, which they place across the mouth of a ceramic pot or a gourd. The sloppy mash is collected in the pot.

There are different ways to press the liquid out, and one of them is by using the interesting Indian tool *tipiti*. The tipiti is a five-foot-long (1.6 meters) cylinder about five inches (12.7 centimeters) across. It is made of bias-woven strips of palm leaf. This combination of material and geometry allows the tipiti to constrict when it is pulled lengthwise, sort of like a giant Chinese finger puzzle.

Grated manioc is stuffed into the tipiti, which is then suspended from a rafter and attached to a hundred-pound weight at its bottom end. Thus constricted, the grated manioc emits a liquid starch, which streams out the bottom of the tipiti into a gourd. The gourds are then stored wet in beautiful baskets kept in the ocas. Now the process of decanting the juice starts. The manioc juice is boiled with fragrant native herbs for many hours in a large ceramic pot over an open fire in order to remove any cyanotic acid.

When the decanting process is done, men remove the pot from the fire and place it in the open air to cool. With great enthusiasm everybody gathers around the pot, and the men pour the cooled liquid into small

individual gourds. Traditionally, they offer it first to the women and then to all the other men present at this social occasion, celebrating the first gift of this magic plant. The rest of the liquid is then stored to be later used in various dishes and beverages. What is left at the bottom of the gourd becomes a viscous, starchy, gumlike product that will be processed separately.

Then the women remove the fiber mass of grated manioc from inside the tipiti and take it to the tribe's *iapuna* (oven) to be dried and roasted. Like all the other utensils used to cook and eat, the women manufacture their own iapuna, which is a large, round earthenware tray on a round base under which a fire is lit.

U sing a tool that resembles a hoe, a woman patiently pushes the fiber slowly in ever-larger circles so the manioc is uniformly roasted. This process of drying and roasting makes the manioc flour, and driving out the water is essential for its long-term storage.

The last step in processing manioc is the making of the tasty tapioca, obtained from the starch collected from the bottom of the gourds that was stored in the baskets.

The wet starch is hand-pressed through a square, woven palm-leaf strainer that forms the starch into little balls.

The strained little balls are collected below on a wooden tray and are brought to the iapuna to be cooked and dried. The minuscule little balls pop with the heat as they release a delicate sweet aroma that impregnates the whole place. This sound is identical to the sound of roasting popcorn. The product of this roasting is tapioca flour, sometimes called *beiju*. Tapioca is used to prepare soups, porridges, and desserts. It is also used to make delicious thin crepes called *tapioquinha,* served for snacks and breakfast.

At the end of this long and careful process, the families have four precious manioc products. These products serve as a base for their food over most of the year. Indeed, the staple the manioc provides is the source of numerous dishes that have made Indian cooking distinctive and unchanged throughout centuries. One dish is *pirão*, a sort of porridge made with the roasted manioc flour, fish broth, and the herb *nhambi,* a kind of coriander; another is *farofa*, a side dish based on manioc flour to which almost any extra food that is handy that day is added and then fried or roasted in the manioc. *Inquitaya* manioc is a mix of hot peppers and a rustic form of salt collected from seawater (this is eaten by the natives living on the coast), and *paçoca* is a pounded dry fishmeal mixed with manioc flour. Then there are soups and stews made with fresh hot peppers and *tucupi,* the unique broth produced with the juice extracted from the manioc with the tipiti.

Other elements of the Indian diet that have so deeply influenced Brazilian cuisine are fish and game, hearts of palm, corn, sweet potatoes, some beans, and, most of all, an extraordinary number of fantastic fruits and hot peppers.

Traditional Cooking

According to Pero Vaz de Caminha (the scribe for the King of Portugal), when the Portuguese arrived in the 1500s, they were amazed with the variety, fragrance, taste, and colors of the fruits they saw in the new land. He also reported extensively about the quality and quantity of red and yellow hot peppers, the popular chilies. These chilies, from the Capsicum baccatum family, are used abundantly in dishes from the Amazon region, and they are commonly used all over Brazil. In Brazil, however, hot spices are usually served on the side so that their use is optional, contrasting with countries like Mexico and India where hot spices are usually already incorporated into the dish and are thus unavoidable.

The heart of the Amazonian Indian house is their barbecue, known by them as the *moquém*. Almost all Europeans, who traveled in Brazil from the sixteenth century on ate meals prepared by the cunhãs (Indian women) on this native barbecue. Again, it was the Frenchman Jean de Lèry who described the moquém in detail:

At each corner of a four-foot-long square, Indians plant a forked pole about three feet high. Then they make a four-foot-square horizontal grid from sticks spaced one inch apart. Vines secure these sticks and then the grid is fixed atop the four poles. Each family has its own moquém. Using selected dry woods to avoid smoke, they light a low fire and slowly start grilling the meats by turning them around every quarter of an hour until they are thoroughly cooked. Since they do not use salt as we do, this is the only way by which they seem to be able to preserve their food (Fernandes 2002).

The moquém, an effective tool used to cook all kinds of foods from game, fish, and fowls to vegetables and fruits, is also extremely efficient in fixing the flavor and color of the food and preserving the food's character.

The cunhãs, praised by the Portuguese as being good cooks, used interesting strategies to grill foods on the moquém. One of them was to wrap the food in large leaves such as the *pacova* (a native banana) and place it on the moquém to be cooked. The travelers of the times claimed the result was truly successful: food not only kept its natural moisture, but the taste was intensified and the leaves could be eaten as well. Interestingly, the natives spread copious amounts of hot peppers on their food that apparently made many Europeans sick to their stomachs.

Another native way of cooking was using clay pots and gourds. The cunhãs prepared soups with the *tucupi*, such as *quinhapira* and *tacacá*, as well as hot alcoholic beverages like *caxiri* in the clay pots.

The gourds, used commonly as eating utensils, have remained popular and are still largely used today. They come from a fruit that grows on a robust vine, and their shape resembles a round squash locals call *cuias*.

During the 1600s, Jesuits traveling in the new land noted in their journals that Brazil's indigenous people had an obvious preference for liquid foods, preferred to eat many small meals a day, and that they intensely disliked salt.

The *tacacá*, a delicious soup served in gourds, is extremely popular today. This typical native dish, that seems not to have equivalent in any other cuisine, is made with tucupi, garlic, the herb *jambu*, dried shrimp, and the starchy manioc flour. By five o'clock in the afternoon, vendors are on the streets in many neighborhoods of Belém and Manaus selling tacacá. Residents have their favorite carts where they stop for their afternoon tacacá.

Belém

In the beautiful city of Belém, one feels transported to another world where tropical temperatures, luxuriant forests, and rivers flowing from everywhere form a remarkable estuary full of all sorts of life!

The docks on the Guamá River date to the late nineteenth century and have been beautifully restored today.

Some of the riverboats coming and going from Belém's docks carry passengers, while others are loaded with fish, vegetables, and fruits coming from distant shores to be delivered to the market Ver o Peso. This astonishing market is the heart of the city of Belém, and as a heart, it seems that it never stops pumping!

As early as three o'clock in the morning, hundreds of large and small boats are tightly packed four deep along the right-angle pier. The boats arrive loaded with a profusion of fish and shellfish, caught in the generous water of the rivers of the Amazon basin, which will be shipped and sold to fish markets in cities such as New York and London

Once there, the fish take on new names: *pargo* becomes Caribbean red snapper, *cioba* is called red tail, and *catuá* is strawberry fish. Hundreds of men work frenetically in the open-air market lifting wooden boxes filled with heavy masses of fish.

Amazingly, they carry the heavy loads skillfully balanced on top of their heads. Walking fast, they take the boxes to be weighed on the old-fashioned nineteenth-century scales along the pier.

Money changes hands rapidly as the traders decide the values of the merchandise of the day. The fish are sold at prices that vary according to the quantity, thus following the old law of supply and demand.

Once the transactions are finished, the strong porters deliver the contents to the numerous trucks that have been waiting across

It is remarkable to follow the ways foods have been disseminated around the world!

When Richard and I are sitting around our Brazilian table with our guests, it is always fun to see their surprised expressions when I tell them that the tapioca flour, so popular around the world, originally came straight from the backyards of Brazilians. As early as the mid-sixteenth century, the Portuguese brought it from Brazil to Goa and Macao, and from there it spread to South Asia, Europe, and the United States. And they are enlightened that even the word "tapioca" is from the tupi language.

Guests are surprised to learn that the Africans who returned home from Brazil in the nineteenth century brought with them some of the dishes that are so popular in Nigeria today. These dishes were created during the slavery period by African women who cooked with native Indian ingredients on Brazilian stoves.

They love to hear that the cashew nut we munch on for snacks and appetizers and that is used in Asian cuisine is the principal part of a fragrant and colorful fruit. The Indians call it acauí, and like the tapioca, it was first taken from Brazil to Africa and India by Portuguese ships.

They are delighted to find out that the chilies so common today in Thai cuisine once came from Amazon Indians' gardens!

the square. These valuable fish are laid on thick beds of ice on the floors of the trucks, thus assuring that, after a long journey, they arrive fresh at their final destination.

Ver o Peso

To the side of the fish market is the late-nineteenth-century building of the Ver o Peso. Considered a historical landmark, it is also the city's icon with its unmistakable two steeple-like towers and iron structure.

In front of the towers are hundreds of stalls, displaying a fantastic array of regional fruit, hot peppers, herbs, and the various manioc products.

The fruit fills the market with an extraordinary variety of colors and aromas. On one side are piles and piles of açaí presented in attractive baskets. Cashew fruit, yellow and red, are beautifully arranged in a circular shape, exhaling their inimitable fragrance.

The grotesque-looking fruit *cupuaçú* is also sold. It is ten inches (25.4 centimeters) long and weighs about two pounds (.9 kilograms), but it has a rich pulp that is used in concocting fine desserts like sorbets and mousses. And from its fatty nuts, it is possible to extract a paste (similar to the cacao), which produces a delicious chocolate!

Enthusiastic merchants give all kinds of information and advice about the products they sell, telling stories and myths that lend a magical touch to the transaction.

A whole section of the Ver o Peso is reserved for the multiplicity of fresh herbs and greens; sometimes used as medicines, they are also indispensable ingredients to the splendid regional dishes. Among the many herbs, the most used are the jambu and a type of coriander called chicória.

The jambu, also known as the watercress of Pará, is an intriguing herb that, besides having a slight bitter taste, gives a funny sensation of numbness in the mouth. The chicória, or Pará coriander, has a similar taste to coriander and its use is essential in the preparation of tucupi.

Ver o Peso also has a series of stands displaying a huge variety of hot peppers of all kinds and colors, from deep red to yellow, pink, green, and purple; each one has a different taste and degree of piquancy, and some are dangerously hot.

Hundreds of bottles of vibrant yellow tucupi are uniformly lined along a counter at the market. Each bottle lists the name of the tucupi producer. It seems that some people will only buy tucupi from a specific source.

The manioc flours—mounds of white, starchy goma; sacs of shiny, roasted yellow and white flour; crunchy tapioca—are all made in the manioc mills across the rivers. It is interesting to observe the local buyers tasting the flours: they put a spoonful in their hand and literally throw it into their mouths. It definitely takes some skill not to have the flour falling all over one's chin and clothes.

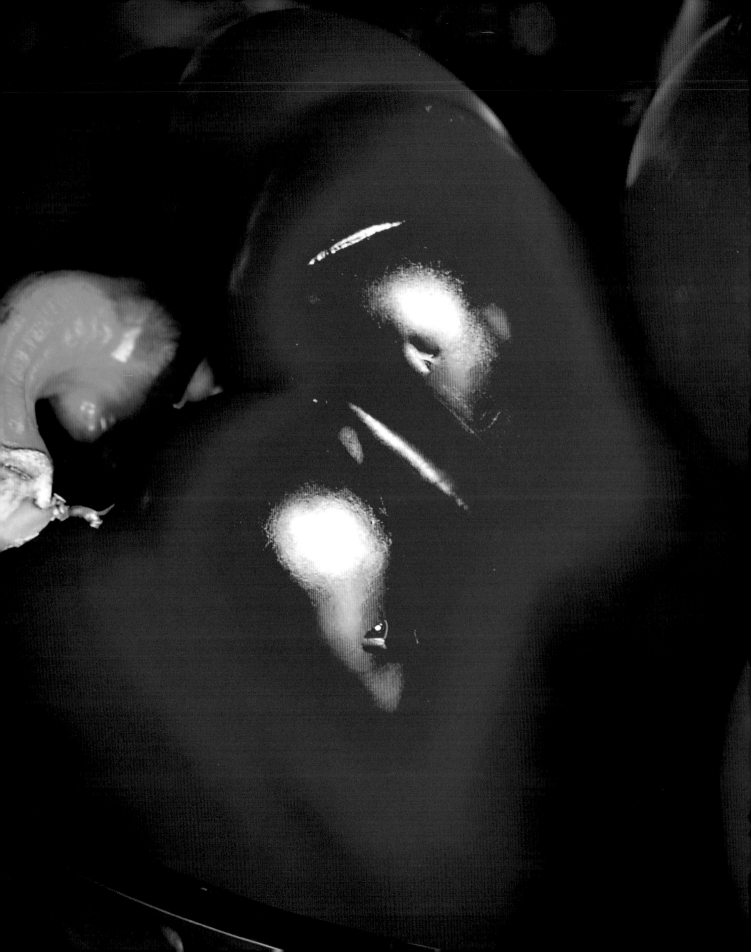

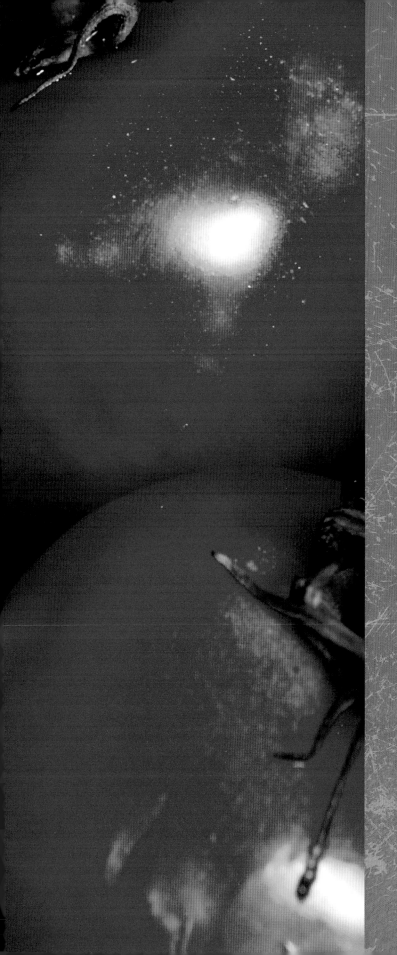

the recipes of the amazon

Brazilian Garden Salad

SERVES 6

VINAIGRETTE
1 tablespoon salt
1 teaspoon black pepper
1 teaspoon nutmeg
2 tablespoons lime juice
5 teaspoons orange flower
  blossom (optional)
Juice from orange sections (below)
1 teaspoon orange zest
6 tablespoons olive oil

SALAD
1 cup peeled and julienned chayote
4 cups lettuce, washed and dried
2 cups watercress, picked, washed
  and dried
1 cup peeled and sectioned
  orange, saving the juice
1 (14-ounce) can hearts of palm,
  drained and cut crosswise in
  $1/2$-inch slices

VINAIGRETTE
1 In a small bowl, mix the salt, pepper, and nutmeg together. Whisk in the lime juice, the orange flower blossom, the juice from the orange sections, and the orange zest until you obtain a homogeneous mixture. Add the olive oil, whisking in vigorously.

SALAD
2 In a medium-size bowl, pour in 3 teaspoons of the vinaigrette and add the chayote. Toss gently. Press to remove the excess and reserve. Proceed in the same way with the lettuce and the watercress, tossing gently.

3 On a large, flat serving dish, spread the rest of the vinaigrette in the center of the dish. Place a pile of the greens in the middle of the dish, making it as high as possible. Arrange the chayote around the greens, and then decorate, alternating the oranges and the hearts of palm on top of the chayote.

4 Pour the remaining dressing around the salad.

Shrimp Soup with Brazil Nut Milk

SERVES 6

4^1/$_2$ cups milk, divided
2 cups shrimp broth, divided
^{1}/$_2$ cup tapioca flour
1 cup Brazil nuts
^{1}/$_2$ cup medium-hot water, divided
2 ripe tomatoes, peeled and
  seeded
1 cup chopped onion, divided (^{1}/$_2$
  cup finely chopped)
^{1}/$_2$ cup peeled, seeded and
  chopped red bell pepper
2 tablespoons olive oil
2 garlic cloves, peeled and
  chopped
2 pounds medium-size shrimp,
  peeled, deveined and washed
1 bouquet garni (2 sprigs parsley,
  1 bay leaf, 2 sprigs scallions)
Salt to taste
1^1/$_2$ teaspoon butter
1 teaspoon achiote powder

1 Heat 1 cup milk and 1 cup shrimp broth. Place the tapioca in a tray and pour the hot liquid over it, mixing gently with a fork. Cover and reserve.

2 Place the nuts in a food processor or blender with just enough hot water to cover them. Process for 2–3 minutes or until it becomes a paste. Place the paste in a clean napkin and place over a glass measuring cup. Pour the remaining hot water over it. With one hand, hold the corners of the napkin together tightly and twist the napkin with the other hand. Twist the napkin as you press the bottom of the napkin where the paste is. Press hard to "milk" the grated Brazil nut. You should get about ^{1}/$_2$ to 1 cup of Brazil nut milk. Reserve.

3 In a food processor or a blender, process the tomatoes, onion, and bell pepper until it turns into a paste.

4 In a medium-size saucepan, warm the olive oil and sauté the garlic until the garlic is lightly golden. Add the shrimp, the processed vegetables, and the bouquet garni. Season with

salt. Stir well and allow to cook about 5 minutes or until the shrimp turns pink. Remove from the heat and reserve.

5 In a stockpot, heat the butter and sauté the ^{1}/$_2$ cup finely chopped onion until soft. Add the rest of the milk and shrimp broth and allow to boil gently while adding the rest of the ingredients.

6 Rub the tapioca mixture between the palms of your hands to crumble it until it becomes tender. Add it slowly to the stockpot, stirring well. Fold in the shrimp with the blended vegetables. Remove bouquet garni. Remove from heat and slowly whisk in the Brazil nut milk. Salt to taste. Pour the soup into 6 serving bowls and sprinkle achiote on top of the soup.

7 Serve at once.

Tacacá (Amazon Soup with Shrimp and Manioc Starch)

SERVES 6

1 bunch escarole
3 bunches jambu or 2 cups watercress, washed and dried
6 cups tucupi
1 tablespoon salt, plus salt for
   boiling
5 garlic cloves, peeled and
   smashed
1 bunch coriander
1 gallon water
1 pound manioc starch (polvilho)
3 hot chilies
2 pounds small shrimp, deveined,
   washed, and blanched

1 Wash and dry the escarole and fresh jambu. Cut in chiffonade and reserve.

2 In a large saucepan, bring the tucupi to a boil. Lower the heat; add the salt, garlic, escarole, and coriander and simmer, covered, for 30 minutes. Reserve.

3 If the jambu is fresh, chop it up and cook with water for $1/2$ hour. (If it is frozen, blanch for 3 minutes.) Drain and press to remove the excess liquid. Reserve.

4 In a stockpot, bring 1 gallon of water and salt to boil. Lower the heat and add the starch slowly through your fingers as you whisk quickly to prevent lumps. This may take 10–15 minutes. Let simmer for another 15 minutes, stirring with a spoon until it turns into a thick porridge. Remove from the stove, but keep warm.

5 In a small serving bowl, crush the chilies with 4 tablespoons tucupi and reserve.

6 To serve, pour $1/2$ ladle of porridge into a gourd or soup bowl; add 1 cup of tucupi and the greens over the porridge and then a couple tablespoons of jambu. Add 5 shrimp and serve with the hot sauce on the side.

Pato no Tucupi (Tucupi Duck Soup)

SERVES 6

2 garlic cloves, peeled
Salt and freshly ground pepper to
   taste
Juice of 2 limes
1 bay leaf, crumbled
2 pounds duck, washed
$1/2$ cup water
5 cups tucupi juice
1/2 cup jambu, sorrel, or watercress, washed and drained
2 cups chicory, washed and
   drained, cut in chiffonade

1 Preheat the oven to 300 degrees F. In a large bowl, crush the garlic, salt, pepper, lime juice, and bay leaf. Add the duck; turn to coat. Cover and marinate in the refrigerator for 2 hours, turning the duck once.

2 Place the duck on a rack in a roasting pan. Pour remaining marinade and $1/2$ cup water into the pan. Place the pan on the lower oven rack and roast for 1 hour or until the skin is crisp and juices run clear when the thigh is pricked with a fork.

3 Cool and cut into 6 pieces, removing the backbone and wing tips.

4 Place the duck in a large nonreactive saucepan and barely cover with water; cook gently for 1 hour over medium heat. Add the tucupi juice and simmer for 30 minutes.

5 Bring a pot of water to a boil and plunge in the jambu or sorrel for 2 minutes. Drain and chop the jambu, and add to the tucupi soup. If using sorrel or watercress, add directly to the tucupi. Remove the duck pieces from the pan, separate the meat from the bones, and shred the meat into small pieces.

6 To serve, take a soupbowl and place $1/2$ cup chicory on the bottom, followed by 5 tablespoons of the shredded duck and 2 cups of the broth.

7 Serve as a first course or as a main dish with rice or Farofa (page 66).

Caldeirada de Peixe do Pará (Pará Fish Stew)

SERVES 6

4 pounds monkfish filets
6 garlic cloves
2 tablespoons chopped cilantro
Juice of 4 limes
3 tablespoons fresh chilies
2 tablespoons salt
6 large new potatoes
1 bunch scallions, divided
1 bunch parsley, divided
8 cups fish stock
6 tablespoons olive oil
1 pound medium-size whole firm tomatoes
1 pound medium-size whole onions, peeled
1 pound shrimp, without shells
6 boiled eggs, peeled
4 sprigs cilantro, for garnish

1 Wash the fish filets with water. In a mortar, crush the garlic, cilantro, lime juice, chilies, and salt. Place the marinade and fish in a bowl, cover, and marinate for 1 hour.

2 Peel the potatoes; place them in a bowl of cold water and reserve. Tie $1/2$ of the scallions and $1/2$ of the parsley together with string to make a bouquet garni.

3 In an earthenware pot or a braiser pan, boil the fish stock, olive oil, and the bouquet garni for 10 minutes.

4 Put in the potatoes, lower the heat, and cook the potatoes for 8 minutes. Distribute the fish, the tomatoes, and the onions around the pan and top with the rest of the herbs. Let it simmer gently, uncovered, for 5 minutes.

5 Arrange the shrimp around the pan and cook for another 5 minutes. Cut the boiled eggs in half, arrange them around the pan, and simmer for another 3 minutes.

6 Serve at once with white rice or Scalded Pirão (page 68). Decorate with cilantro sprigs.

Amazon-Style Fish

SERVES 6

TOMATO SAUCE

2 tablespoons vegetable oil
1 cup chopped onions
6 garlic cloves, peeled and
  chopped
3 tablespoons chopped cilantro
Salt and pepper to taste
1 pound tomatoes, peeled,
  seeded, and quartered or 1
  (16-ounce) can whole tomatoes,
  quartered
2 teaspoons Tabasco sauce or 1
  malagueta pepper, crushed

FISH

8 teaspoons salt, divided
2 tablespoons lime juice
6 cups water, divided
6 large shrimp, peeled but with
  tails on
6 squares of banana leaf (found in
  Asian food stores) or 1–2 whole
  young banana leaves (if using a
  whole fish)
3 pounds whole tile fish, boned
  and open in butterfly (head and
  tail on) or 6 fish filets
Farofa (page 66)
Grilled Bananas (page 67)
Onion Confit (page 66)

TOMATO SAUCE

1 In a medium saucepan, heat the vegetable oil and sauté the onions over medium-low heat until they soften. Add the garlic, mixing well, and then the cilantro. Stir a couple of times. Season with the salt and pepper. Add the tomatoes and the Tabasco or malagueta pepper. Cook for 3 minutes and set aside.

FISH

2 Preheat the oven to 325 degrees F. In a small bowl, combine 4 teaspoons salt and the lime juice. Reserve.

3 In a small saucepan, bring to boil 2 cups water with 4 teaspoons salt. Place 2 shrimp at a time in the pan and cook them for 2–3 minutes. Remove from the pan and immerse in ice water. Drain and reserve.

4 If using fresh banana leaves, in a medium-size frying pan, boil 4 cups water. Using tongs, carefully immerse one banana leaf square and blanch for1–2 minutes. Remove and strain. The leaf is now shiny and green. Repeat with other leaves and reserve.

5 If using a whole banana leaf, pass it rapidly over an open flame until the leaf turns shiny and soft.

6 Place the banana leaf open on the counter and sprinkle with 1 teaspoon of the salted lime juice. Place the fish filet on top of the banana leaf and

sprinkle again with another teaspoon of the salted lime juice. Using a dessert spoon, spread the tomato sauce $\frac{1}{2}$ inch wide lengthwise in the center of the filet. On top of that, build a lengthwise mound of farofa. Cut a couple of pieces of grilled banana and place them on top of the farofa. Alternate with 2 onion confit; press down slightly with the palm of the hand. Gently roll up the fish so the contents remain in place. It helps to cup your hands around the side of the roll and press in as though you were making a snowball. Fold the banana leaf around the fish as if you were wrapping a present, and pin each end with a toothpick.

7 If you are using a whole fish, you need a large banana leaf. Place the fish open on top of the banana leaf. Spread 2–3 tablespoons of salted lime juice on the leaf and place the whole fish on the leaf. Fill the fish in the same way as described above. Close the fish and wrap it with the banana leaf, tying it with a piece of string or using a toothpick.

8 Place the wrapped fish in a baking dish. Pour 1 cup water on the bottom of the pan and bake for 20 minutes, or 30 minutes if making a whole fish.

9 To serve, open the banana leaf, folding it under the fish filet. Place 1 teaspoon of the tomato sauce on top of the fish. Carefully place a medium-size shrimp encircling the tomato sauce. Place 1 tablespoon of farofa on the plate, encircling the fish, and beside it place 2 grilled bananas and 2 onion confit. Serve with malagueta sauce on the side.

Shrimp Juquitaya

SERVES 6

PASTE

$^1/_2$ teaspoon coarse salt
6 teaspoons urucum or achiote
$^1/_2$ teaspoon cayenne
$^1/_2$ teaspoon malagueta pepper,
    seeded
1 tablespoon olive oil
$^1/_2$ teaspoon lime juice

SHRIMP

1 pound large shrimp, peeled,
    deveined, and washed (leave the
    tail on)
3 pounds pumpkin
2 cups water
1 tablespoon salt
1 cup orange juice
6 pieces orange peel
$^1/_2$ cup butter
4 tablespoons olive oil, divided
3 tablespoons lime juice, divided
3 cups watercress, picked, washed,
    and dried, for decoration
Salt and pepper to taste
6 teaspoons urucum or achiote,
    for garnish

PASTE

1 In a mortar, grind together salt, urucum or achiote, cayenne, and malagueta pepper. Add the olive oil and lime juice and mix, making a paste.

SHRIMP

2 Rub the shrimp with the paste and let marinate for 1 hour.

3 Cut a circle 1$^1/_2$ inch wide from the largest part of the pumpkin. In a braiser pan, boil enough salted water to cover the pumpkin ring, and cook the pumpkin ring for 8 minutes. Drain the pumpkin. Clean the inner part of the circle, removing any fiber that has remained from the cooking process.

4 Cut the rest of the pumpkin into large chunks. Bring water, salt, orange juice, and orange peel to a boil in a large saucepan and cook the pumpkin pieces until they become soft. Drain and save 1 cup of the liquid. Peel the pumpkin and, using a potato masher, mash the pumpkin to make a purée. Fold in the butter, add some of the cooking liquid, and beat with a spoon until it becomes smooth. Keep warm.

5 In a skillet, heat 2 tablespoons oil and sear the shrimp on both sides for 3–4 minutes. In the same skillet, add 2 tablespoons lime juice and deglaze the pan, shaking a couple of times. Keep it warm and reserve.

6 Place the pumpkin circle in the middle of an attractive plate. Fill the interior of the circle with the purée and arrange the grilled shrimp around the circle.

7 Toss the watercress with 1 tablespoon lime juice, 2 tablespoons olive oil, salt, and pepper and arrange it around the pumpkin circle.

8 Sprinkle achiote or urucum around the plate and serve at once.

Fish Brochette with Pineapple

SERVES 6

2 pounds fish steaks (yellow tail,
    hake, or sea wolf)
2 tablespoons urucum or achiote
2 tablespoons coarse salt
4 tablespoons olive oil
1 medium-size pineapple
6 skewers

1 Remove the skins from the fish and cut each fish steak into 2-inch squares. Reserve and keep cold.

2 In a small bowl, mix the urucum with the salt and olive oil.

3 Peel the pineapple and cut into 4 pieces, lengthwise. Take out the core and cut the pineapple into 2-inch cubes.

4 In a large bowl, toss the fish squares with the seasoned oil. Drain the fish and reserve any leftover oil. Skewer the fish and the pineapple, alternating the cubes.

5 Place the skewers in a barbecue preheated to 300 degrees F. Grill for 4 minutes. Before turning the skewers, brush them with the remaining oil. When the fish is cooked, serve the brochettes with Farofa (page 66) or Manioc with Sautéed Onions (page 67).

Stuffed Tomatoes with Manioc Flour and Cashew Nuts

SERVES 4

2 large tomatoes, ripe
2 teaspoons sugar
$1/2$ cup cashew nuts, roasted
$1^1/2$ cups Farofa (page 66)
$4^1/2$ tablespoons olive oil, divided
$1/3$ cup crumbled blue cheese
$1/2$ cup scallions, divided ($1/4$ cup chopped finely)
1 cup watercress and arugula, washed and dried
Salt and pepper to taste

1 Wash and dry the tomatoes. Cut off a small slice from the top of each tomato. Place tomatoes cut-side down on the cutting board.

2 Using the point of a paring knife in a vertical position, make a circular incision $1/2$ inch deep and 2 inches wide. You should end up with 2 nice conical tomato pieces with a point at the end. Reserve for decoration. Core the tomatoes.

3 Sprinkle the inside of the tomatoes with sugar and turn them upside down on a plate. The tomatoes will release some water.

4 Select 4 beautiful cashew nuts and save them for decoration. Coarsely crush the rest of the cashew nuts and reserve.

5 Just before you finish cooking the farofa, mix in 3 tablespoons olive oil, the crumbled cheese, the crushed cashew nuts, and $1/4$ cup finely chopped scallions. Mix well and reserve.

6 Turn the tomatoes, place them on the counter, and sprinkle with salt. Using a spoon, fill each tomato with $1/2$ of the farofa mixture, pressing lightly. Top with the rest of the farofa mixture, a whole cashew nut, and a couple of pieces of scallion. Arrange on a salad plate with the tomato in the center.

7 In a medium-size bowl, toss the watercress and arugula with remaining olive oil, salt, and pepper. Arrange around the tomatoes. Place round tomato top by the side.

Onion Confit

SERVES 6

5$^1/_2$ cups water, divided
3 cups small yellow whole onions
1 tablespoon vegetable oil
6 tablespoons butter
5 teaspoons salt

1 Bring 5 cups water to boil in a pot and blanch the onions for 2 minutes. When they are cool enough to handle, peel the onions and reserve.

2 Heat oil and butter in a heavy skillet over low heat. Place the onions in the skillet and turn them as they become golden, shaking the pan constantly. Add more butter if needed. Keep shaking the skillet to move the onions around in order to make them golden. It will take around 15 minutes.

3 When the onions are golden and cooked, turn off the heat and let the skillet cool. Pour $^1/_2$ cup water and the salt into the skillet and simmer, shaking the skillet well and scraping the bottom of the pan. Let it cool completely and then place the onions in a jar. Cover onions with the liquid from the skillet. Refrigerate up to 3 weeks.

Farofa

SERVES 6

4 tablespoons olive oil or butter
4 garlic cloves, finely chopped
2 cups manioc flour (preferably the yellow kind)
Salt and pepper to taste

1 In a medium-size skillet, heat the oil or butter over low heat and sauté the garlic. When the garlic is soft, pour the manioc flour through your fingers as you stir slowly, mixing it with the butter.

2 When all the fat is absorbed by the flour, gently mix with a spatula, moving the flour from one side to the other to roast it. The farofa is ready when it changes color from light yellow to a more vivid yellow. Season with salt and pepper.

Grilled Bananas

8 bananas, firm but not green
2 tablespoons vegetable oil
4 tablespoons butter
OR
6 tablespoons olive oil

1 Peel the bananas. Place a banana on a cutting board and, using one hand to secure it, gently slice the banana in half lengthwise with a sharp knife. Do the same with the other bananas. Reserve.

2 In a heavy skillet, warm the vegetable oil and butter or the olive oil. When it starts foaming, place 2 halves of the banana at a time in the skillet and grill on one side for 3–4 minutes or until golden brown. Turn the banana gently with a spatula and grill the other side.

3 Remove the bananas from the skillet and place them in a serving dish.

4 Serve at once or heat in the oven on medium-high heat, covered with foil, for 5 minutes.

Manioc with Sautéed Onions

SERVES 6

2 pounds manioc, peeled (fresh or
   frozen)
1 gallon water
3 tablespoons salt
6 tablespoons butter
2 cups julienned onion
Black pepper to taste
2 tablespoons finely chopped
   parsley

1 Cut the peeled manioc into 4-inch cubes. In a large pan, boil water with salt. When it comes to a high boil, place the manioc pieces in the pan. Lower the heat to medium-high and cook the manioc, covered, until they become soft but not to the point of dismantling. Remove the manioc from the pan, reserving 1 cup of the cooking liquid. Keep the manioc warm and covered with some of the cooking liquid.

2 Place the butter in a large sauté pan and sauté the onions until they turn soft and transparent. Add the cooked manioc to the pan and shake a couple of times to coat the pieces with the butter and the onion. Add the reserved cooking liquid and adjust for salt, if necessary. Arrange the manioc pieces in a serving dish and cover with the onion and the sauce. Sprinkle with black pepper and chopped parsley.

3 Serve as a side dish with meats, poultry, and fish.

Pirão Cozido (Cooked Manioc Flour Porridge)

SERVES 4

2 tablespoons vegetable oil
$1/2$ cup chopped onion
4 garlic cloves, chopped
$1/2$ cup chopped red bell pepper
$1/2$ cup chopped tomato
1 cup scraps of fish
Salt to taste
2 cups of fish broth
1 cup water
$3/4$ cup manioc flour
$1/4$ cup chopped cilantro

1 In a medium saucepan, heat the oil and sauté the onion and then the garlic. Stir. Add bell pepper, tomato, and fish, mixing all the ingredients. Season with salt and let it cook for 3 minutes. Remove from heat and place in food processor, adding the fish broth little by little. Process until all the ingredients are well blended.

2 In a medium bowl, mix together the water and the manioc flour.

3 In a medium-size saucepan, place the processed sauce over low heat and gently pour the dissolved manioc into the pan and whisk well. Simmer for 5–8 minutes, stirring constantly.

4 Place the pirão in a serving bowl and sprinkle with chopped cilantro.

Pirão Escaldado (Scalded Manioc Porridge)

SERVES 4

6 cups fish broth
4 cups manioc flour
Salt to taste
$1/4$ cup chopped cilantro

1 Heat the fish broth but do not boil. Place the broth in a shallow bowl and pour the manioc flour slowly through your fingers into the center of the bowl. Mix with a fork, making circles until the flour becomes wet as it absorbs the liquid, about 2–3 minutes. Salt to taste and sprinkle with chopped cilantro.

2 This is a side dish served with stews. It can also be prepared on individual plates. In this case, each person makes his or her own pirão.

Açaí Mousse

SERVES 6

¹/₂ cup plus 2 tablespoons cold
   water, divided
2 teaspoons unflavored gelatin
4 eggs, separated
2 tablespoons lime juice
³/₄ cup sugar
1 cup frozen açaí pulp
2 tablespoons açaí liqueur
Pinch of salt
2 tablespoons confectioners' sugar
6 sprigs mint, for garnish

1 Place ¹/₂ cup water in a bowl and sprinkle the gelatin over it. Let sit for 5 minutes so the gelatin expands. Place the egg yolks in a separate bowl and beat them vigorously. Whisk in 2 table-spoons water as you continue to beat. Add the lime juice and keep whisking until it foams and becomes white.

2 Place the gelatin mixture in a medium-size saucepan over low heat, mixing with a spoon until it dissolves. Add the sugar all at once and mix well to combine all the ingredients. Slowly add the egg yolk mixture, whisking well to prevent the eggs from curdling. Let simmer gently until it foams. Turn off the heat and keep whisking for 3 more minutes.

3 Pour the mixture into a bowl and allow to cool for 10 minutes.

4 Blend the açaí pulp with the liqueur.

5 When the gelatin mixture has cooled, fold in the açaí mixture, gently mixing them together. Place the bowl in the freezer for 15 minutes or until the sides of the açaí congeal and the center of the açaí is soft.

6 Beat the egg whites with a pinch of salt into a stiff, shiny peak. Add the confectioners' sugar and beat again for 10 seconds. Take the açaí bowl out of the freezer. Gently fold ¹/₃ of the beaten egg whites into the açaí mixture, mak-ing circular motions with a spatula. Add another ¹/₃ of the egg whites and fold in gently. Now, reverse the process and slowly pour the açaí mixture into the bowl with the egg whites and fold in the same way.

7 Take 6 wine glasses or serving bowls and distribute the mousse equally. Refrigerate for 1 hour and garnish with mint sprigs.

Brazil Nut Cookies

YIELDS 35

¹/₄ pound Brazil nuts
¹/₂ cup butter, softened
¹/₂ cup sugar, plus 1 cup to coat
   the cookies
¹/₂ cup flour
¹/₂ cup cornmeal

1 Grate the nuts and reserve.

2 In a large bowl, mix the butter with ¹/₂ cup sugar. In another large bowl, combine the flour and nuts with the cornmeal. Add the combined dry ingredients to the first bowl and work well with both hands to mix the ingre-dients until a large ball is formed.

3 Preheat the oven to 375 degrees F. Cover a cookie sheet with parchment

paper (do not grease the cookie sheet). Place 1 cup sugar on a plate.

4 Roll a tablespoon of cookie dough into a ball the size of a large straw-berry. Roll the cookies in the sugar and arrange them in a row on the cookie sheet.

5 Bake for 10 minutes or until they are light golden brown. Serve the cookies at room temperature.

Pudim de Tapioca (Caramelized Tapioca Flan)

SERVES 8

2/3 cup unsweetened coconut milk
1/2 cup milk
1 1/4 cup tapioca flour
5 whole eggs
1 (12-ounce) can condensed milk
1 tablespoon butter
1 2/3 cup cream

CARAMEL
2 cups sugar
4 tablespoons water

1 In a small saucepan, heat the coconut milk and milk. Place the tapioca flour in a tray and pour the hot milk on top of it. Using a fork, gently make a couple of lines in order to allow the liquid to go through the tapioca grains (do not mix it). Let it soak for 2 hours.

2 Using an electric beater, beat the eggs vigorously until they foam. Add the condensed milk and then the butter. As you continue beating, add the cream and finally the soaked tapioca.

3 For the caramel: Place the sugar and water in a saucepan over low heat and simmer the sugar slowly, watching closely so it doesn't burn. When it begins to turn a golden color, turn off the heat. Take an ovenproof mold large enough to hold 5 cups and coat it completely with the caramel. Set it aside.

4 Preheat the oven to 350 degrees F. Gently pour the tapioca batter into the caramelized mold. Place a larger baking pan in the oven and carefully pour 6 cups of boiling water into it. Gently place the caramelized mold with batter in the center of the pan and bake for 50 minutes. Check doneness by placing a toothpick in the center of the flan: if it comes out dry, the flan is done. Allow to cool.

5 Invert the mold onto a serving plate and allow caramel from the mold to flow over top of the flan.

Cupuaçú Ice Cream

SERVES 8

1 pound frozen cupuaçú pulp (you may use any other frozen tropical fruit pulp)
2 1/4 cups condensed milk
2 tablespoons lime juice

1 In a blender, combine the frozen pulp and the condensed milk. Blend for 3 to 4 minutes, stopping a couple of times to unblock the frozen pulp if necessary. Add the lime juice and blend some more.

2 Pour the mixture into a transparent serving dish or stainless steel tray and place in the freezer for a couple of hours. Serve with fruit salad, cakes, or ladyfinger cookies.

Tapioca Blinis

SERVES 8

$3/4$ cup tapioca
2 egg yolks, lightly beaten
3 egg whites, lightly beaten
$4^1/2$ tablespoons coconut milk
$1^1/2$ cups milk
$4^1/2$ tablespoons cachaça
2 tablespoons sugar
2 tablespoons butter

1 Spread tapioca evenly in a thin layer on a medium-size tray.

2 In a medium bowl, combine the egg yolks, egg whites, and coconut milk. Mix well and reserve.

3 In a small saucepan, bring the milk, cachaça, and sugar to a quick boil. To temper the eggs, add $1/4$ cup of the milk to the bowl with the eggs and whisk. Gently pour the tempered eggs into the saucepan, whisking rapidly.

4 Pour the liquid over the tapioca and, using a fork, make circles around it so the liquid soaks in totally (do not mix). Cover and let sit for 2 hours.

5 Cut 3-inch circles in the tapioca. Just before serving, heat a medium-size heavy skillet. When the skillet is hot, place a dollop of butter in it. Using a spatula, place 2 circles at a time in the skillet. Sear the tapioca blinis on both sides until they turn golden.

6 Place 1 blini on an individual plate and serve immediately with ice cream or sorbet. Garnish with flowers or mint.

Pineapple Aluá

SERVES 8

1 medium-size ripe pineapple
8 cups water
Sugar (optional)
Mint leaves

1 Wash the pineapple well. Remove the skin by cutting $1/4$ inch into the fruit so the peel has a layer of the fruit. Place the pineapple peels inside an attractive transparent jar and add water. Mix lightly and let sit for 3 hours.

2 Cut out the core of the pineapple and cut the pineapple into small squares. Place the pineapple in a blender and process until it becomes liquid.

3 Using a jar and strainer, strain the processed pineapple by pressing hard to get the maximum out of the fruit. Add sugar, if using it.

4 Pour the juice into ice cube trays and freeze.

5 To serve, pour the strained pineapple water into tall glasses, add 1 or 2 pineapple ice cubes, and garnish with mint leaves.

The Cooking of Bahía

African culture has a decisive presence in Brazil: it was part of the past, it has sculpted the present, and it has built a permanent path into the future.

It is in the city of São Salvador da Bahía (known to all as simply "Salvador"), in the state of Bahía, that the wonderful African culture has blossomed in all aspects of life. It is here that we can see most directly how these African roots are at the core of the dishes of the region.

To connect to Bahían cooking, it is important to know something of its history and traditions. By the end of the sixteenth century, tens of thousands of Africans were brought to Brazil as slaves to work in agriculture, sugarcane plantations, mines, and as house servants. The African slaves were from several regions of Africa including Angola, Ivory Coast, Sierra Leone, and Cape Verde, and had diverse linguistic and cultural backgrounds. A common denominator, however, for a great part of them, was that they came from well-developed and well-organized societies. Their people had been part of great empires with armies of warriors known for having fought battles using complex war strategies. In addition to being lethal, their weapons were finely painted and sculpted.

The splendor of Africans' artistic ceremonies, either to honor their kings or their gods, had motivated the creation of musical instruments, decorative objects, and textiles, as well as chants and collective dances they performed during celebrations.

Africans knew irrigation methods, made wine from the palm tree, and raised cattle and domesticated animals, but, most of all, they were excellent hunters. Hunting was not only an occupation for males, but also a form of amusement and a symbol of pride and dignity.

Their diet included game; cereals such as rice, which they learned how to cook from the Berbers; yams, cooked or baked to accompany fish and meats; and flour, which was used to make cakes. Salt was obtained from palm tree ashes, and, last but not least, the Africans used palm oil and a large variety of hot peppers to flavor their dishes.

Their cooking methods included baking, barbecuing, and smoking, but not frying, which they did not learn until later from the Portuguese.

The Africans mastered techniques to work the leather, metals, wood, bone, and ivory with which they made all kinds of elegant objects designed for everyday domestic use.

Abruptly taken away from their land and torn apart from their culture, the captured slaves in Africa were thrown into the darkness of ships' galleys, sailing toward even more darkness as they crossed the ocean to an unknown destiny. These people had to leave behind everything they had, losing forever their status and, at times, their humanity.

In the obscurity of the ships' galleys during those terrible crossings, the Africans chanted and prayed as they held desperately to their respective religions, fostering and creating a new way to worship their gods, or *orixás*.

Indeed, this spirituality that could not be taken away from them flourished later in the new land, where the worshipers searched for and found a common ground for their religious needs.

After sailing for months, the ships carrying the slaves landed in ports all along the coast of Brazil but in higher numbers in Salvador. Most Africans brought there were from the Sudanese region of West Africa. This concentration in Salvador of African slaves with a homogeneous cultural background was an important factor in shaping an Afro-Brazilian culture with clear and dominant traits that has prevailed throughout centuries all over Brazil.

Among these dominant cultural traditions, religion became the most important of all. In fact, it was in their religion that the different groups found shelter and developed a new set of cultural paradigms.

The first new paradigm seems to have started at the ports, where Catholic chaplains were waiting for the ships carrying the African slaves.

Upon the arrival of slave ships, chaplains began teaching the slaves how to pray in Latin and proceeded to baptize them, giving them Christian names and introducing the converted to a new iconography.

The Africans who had held onto their orixás—representing the forests, rivers, oceans, and sky—began to mingle their familiar entities with the new Catholic God and Catholic saints, to the extent that each orixá came to have a corresponding "namesake" in the Catholic religion.

When the slaves celebrated the Catholic rites, their performance included the chants and the dances of their native lands, as well as the artistic aspect inherent in African religious expression. The Candomblé religion, with a few variations, is a solid result of all of these forces.

For me, Brazil where I grew up, would have been less interesting without its African influence.

It would have lacked the soothing lullabies that sent me slowly and peacefully to my night dreams; I wouldn't have heard the bewitching stories that filled my days with fantasies replete with mysteries from distant lands. I cannot imagine my childhood without the rhymes and songs we children recited as we moved our bodies through the African rhythm and went around holding hands in a circle. I would have missed some wonderful street games with the African set of symbols and rules that taught me and helped me to practice some important social skills that I have used everyday since then.

We wouldn't have participated in the celebration of *ebejês* (orixá children), such as the twins Cosme and Damião. Every September 27, fruits and delicious hand-made candies and cookies were given to us children by all the adults we happened to cross that day. I particularly loved finding images of these adorable orixá children in the houses we visited on that day. There were always lit candles and the typical offerings: a ceramic bowl containing *caruru* (a dish made with okra) and another one with water. We were told that Cosme and Damião protect the children and help people find lost objects. I found this very convenient—what a good feeling to know that our human lapses fall in good hands!

Without this African culture, we Brazilians wouldn't have adopted the most popular celebration of the year throughout our entire country on December 31. On that day, we dress in white and prepare our set of gifts to Yemanjá, a powerful African orixá who lives in the ocean. She loves to receive gifts such as white flowers, blue ribbons, refined perfumes, mirrors, combs, face powder, jewelry, champagne, and fruits. We arrange all the gifts carefully on a charming model version of the *saveiros*, the graceful wooden fishing schooners that also carried freight in Brazil before the age of diesel. We think about what we will say to her, and then we thank her for the year just ended and we ask her graces and favors for the new year about to begin. Just before sunset, thousands of people walk to the beaches to send offerings to this beautiful lady.

As part of the remembrance, we dig a shallow hole in the sand, place our candles inside, and light them. Close to midnight, we approach the water with our saveiro filled with gifts and we wait for a good wave to position it on the water. The surf intensifies and roars, the saveiro goes up and down . . . we pace and hope. If Yemanjá accepts our offerings, the waves will take the little boat out and away from the shore. After floating for a while, the boat will then sink and spread its precious offerings over Yemanjá's world.

Before we head back home, we dive into Yemanjá's waters, coming full circle as we ourselves become another gift to her.

I am amazed to see that this fantastic African culture that has developed since colonial times in Brazil is so resilient and rooted in our daily lives. How can one conceive of Brazil without African culture? It would have been a Brazil without its unmistakable music that has spread into a variety of rhythms throughout the regions. It would have been a Brazil without the dances inspired by those rhythms such as the samba with its variations, the *capoeira*, the *maracatu*, the *frevo*; a Brazil without a great part of its unique oral traditions and literature; a Brazil without the joy, exuberance, and sensuality of its people; a Brazil without the religion, the syncretism, the colorful ceremonies. And of course, it would be a Brazil without the Afro-Bahían unctuous dishes that make our cuisine richer and more tantalizing.

Once in Salvador, we feel magically immersed in the realm of the syncretism of Brazilian Africa among blacks, whites, and mulattoes. We are surrounded by dozens of white baroque churches cohabiting with the tan-tan drums of the Candomblé world. Africa penetrates us through all of our senses, imposing its rhythm on our body and our soul. During the warm evenings in São Salvador of Bahía, we may follow the language of the many drums and the tolling of the bells,

all talking to each other and transforming Salvador into a holy city.

This vibrant city becomes the stage for the rites of the Candomblé religion when Africa and Brazil seem to no longer be separated by the ocean. The public ceremony starts with the sounds of the *atabaques* (three drums) spreading from the room to the city like a deluge until it reaches Africa. These sounds make an irresistible invitation to the African orixás to cross the ocean in order to participate in the celebration. The music is indispensable for the ceremony.

According to tradition, during a Candomblé ceremony there may be different orixás coming from Africa to participate with the worshipers here, and depending on the appearances, the ceremony will have a different characteristic and style.

Who are these orixás who keep their "residence" in Africa and travel back and forth to Brazil?

Oxalá is the father of all orixás and uses the colors white and silver; Friday is his day. That day, it is common to see people dressed entirely in white. Most of the time, Oxalá is the first one to appear at a Candomblé ceremony. His favorite foods are goat and sugarcane.

Xangô represents the tempest, lightning, and thunder, and Wednesday is his day. His colors are white and red, and he carries an ax with wings. He likes to eat lamb, rooster, and, most of all, *amalá*, an okra-based dish.

Ogún, the god of iron, wears clothes of a beautiful deep blue. At times he carries a sword and at other times, agriculture tools.

He likes to eat goat meat cooked with palm oil and also popcorn. When he dances, Ogún makes movements that resemble a fight.

Oxossí's colors are green, blue, and red, and he is the god of the hunt. He carries a sword and is accompanied by a dragon; Thursday is his day, as it is for Ogún. Among his favorite foods are those made with pork and chicken.

Among the female orixás is Oxúm, who is more of a young girl than a woman. She holds a fan and also likes to have toys around her. She represents springs and streams, and her color is a radiant gold yellow. She likes chicken xim-xim and dried shrimp served with dendê-scented manioc flour.

Then there is Nanã, the mother of the orixás, who wears light blue and white. She dances like an old woman, pretending that she is carrying a baby. She likes to eat dishes cooked with lamb, chicken, and acaçá, a side dish similar to polenta and made with white rice.

Yansã is Xangô's wife and for that reason is evoked during huge storms. She wears red and white and carries a sword. Her favorite foods are acarajé and abará, both made with a pea-paste base.

And finally, there is Yemanjá, the most beautiful and voluptuous of all the female orixás, the queen of the ocean where she lives. She appears in an attractive, long, draped blue and white gown, and she wears necklaces made of shells. Her looks suggest that of the Virgin Mary, and, as in the Catholic religion, she is also celebrated on December 8. She likes to eat duck, acaçá, and chicken.

Necklaces and ribbons of a variety of colors are part of the scene in markets of Salvador, where worshipers get their personal orixá's ornaments. Each orixá is also believed to have its own expertise and is able, when consulted, to influence certain domains of life such as love, money, power, and health.

The ceremony accelerates with more music, chants, and dances and continues through the night, culminating with the distribution of the many dishes prepared that morning for the orixás from the kitchens of the iabassés, older women who hold that responsibility and who are fantastic cooks. This time, the cortège is composed of younger women carrying the tantalizing dishes. They then respectfully arrange them around a straw mat placed in the center of the room. The aroma impregnates the whole room, and the sight of bounteous earthenware containing the blessed orixás' foods is mouthwatering.

Like all of the other gods, the African orixás are gourmand and gourmet!

the recipes of bahía

Abará

SERVES 6

1 pound dried black-eyed peas
1/4 pound dry-smoked shrimp or small fresh shrimp
1 medium onion, chopped
1 malagueta or chili pepper, mashed
Salt and pepper to taste
1/4 cup dendê oil
6 banana leaves, cut in squares
12 toothpicks

1 Soak the peas in water and cover for 6 hours, changing the water every hour. Drain the peas and cover them again with fresh water. Rub the peas between the palms of your hands to remove the outer skin. Allow the peas to settle and the skins to float to the top. Skim off the skins and drain the peas. Soak the peas again and proceed the same way until all the skins are removed.

2 If using dry shrimp, soak them for 1 hour. Drain and chop them coarsely. If using fresh shrimp, wash, drain, and chop them coarsely. Reserve.

3 In a food processor or blender, purée the peas and chopped onion in two batches. Place the pea purée in a mixing bowl; combine this purée with the malagueta pepper, salt, and pepper. Using a wooden spoon, beat the resulting paste rapidly until it starts to foam.

4 Add the dendê oil, mixing well until it becomes a homogenous mixture. Fold in the shrimp and reserve.

5 Place a square of banana leaf on a flat surface. Arrange 6 tablespoons of the pea mixture in the center of the square and wrap tightly (it will look like a small package). Secure the sides with 2 toothpicks.

6 Bring 2 quarts of water to boil in a stockpot. Place the abarás in the pot and boil them for 8 minutes or until they rise to the top. Serve with hot pepper sauce on the side.

BANANA LEAVES

7 Select 6 young, medium-size banana leaves. (If the leaf is dark green, it means that the leaf is old and it will break in the process. A light green leaf will be more pliable.) Wipe the leaves with a damp cloth. Cut a 12 x 12-inch square from each leaf.

8 Boil water in a medium-size sauté pan. Using tongs, immerse the squares in water for 5 seconds. Remove from the pan and place on a rack to dry.

9 Cover the banana leaves with a wet kitchen towel. The blanched leaves may be kept wrapped in the vegetable section of the refrigerator for up to 4 days.

Acarajé Soufflé

SERVES 6

1 pound dried black-eyed peas
1 medium onion, quartered
1 preserved malagueta chile
   pepper, mashed
Salt and pepper to taste
2 tablespoons butter, softened
4 tablespoons bread crumbs
6 egg whites
6 medium-size shrimp, peeled,
   deveined, and cut in half,
   lengthwise

1 Place the peas in a large bowl and soak them for 4 to 6 hours, changing the water as many times as needed.

2 Drain the peas and cover again with fresh water. Rub the peas between the palms of your hands to remove the outer skin. Allow the peas to settle and the skins to float to the top. Skim off the skins and drain the peas. Repeat this process until all the skins are removed.

3 In a food processor or blender, purée the peas with the quartered onion, in two batches.

4 In a mixing bowl, combine the purée with the malagueta pepper, salt, and pepper. Using a wooden spoon, beat the pea paste until it starts to foam.

5 Preheat the oven to 400 degrees F. Place a cookie sheet on the lowest rack in the oven.

6 Coat a soufflé mold or 6 ramekins with butter and sprinkle with bread crumbs.

7 Beat the egg whites with a pinch of salt to a peak. With a spatula, gently fold 1 cup of the egg white into the pea paste. Reverse the procedure and pour this mixture into the bowl with the rest of the egg white and gently fold again.

8 Gently fill $\frac{1}{2}$ of the mold or ramekins with the pea mixture. Place half of one shrimp in the center and fill the container to the top with the pea mixture. Place the other shrimp half carefully on top of the mixture.

9 Bake it for 8–10 minutes and serve immediately with a dendê-scented béchamel.

Acarajé

1 pound dried black-eyed peas
1 medium onion, quartered
1 preserved malagueta chile
  pepper, mashed
Salt and pepper to taste
4 cups vegetable oil
2 tablespoons dendê oil (optional)
4 cups Dendê-scented Béchamel
  Sauce (page 99)
3/4 pound medium-size shrimp,
  deveined and washed
Parsley sprigs, for garnish

1 Cover the peas with water and soak for 4 to 6 hours, changing the water as many times as needed. Drain the peas and cover with fresh water. Rub the peas between the palms of your hands to remove the outer skin. Allow the peas to settle and the skins to float to the top. Skim off the skins and drain the peas. Repeat this process until all the skins are removed.

2 In a food processor or blender, purée the peas with the quartered onion, in two batches.

3 In a mixing bowl, combine the purée with the malagueta pepper, salt, and pepper. Using a wooden spoon, beat the pea paste until it starts to foam.

4 Using two oval spoons, form some of the mixture into an egg-shaped oval.

5 Heat the vegetable oil and dendê oil in a heavy, medium-size saucepan until very hot. (You may place a match in the oil. When the match lights, the oil is hot enough to deep fry.) Place 2 acarajés at a time in the pan and fry, turning them over once. Remove from the pan and drain on a paper towel. Keep warm.

6 Serve as is or with vatapá and malagueta sauce or a béchamel. If serving with the béchamel, add the shrimp to the béchamel and cook for 3–4 minutes.

7 To serve, place 1/4 cup of the béchamel or the vatapá in the center of an individual serving plate. Distribute 3–4 acarajés around the béchamel and garnish with parsley sprigs.

Ginger-Honey Salad

SERVES 6

GINGER-HONEY DRESSING
4 teaspoons salt
2 teaspoons black pepper
2 tablespoons finely chopped fresh ginger
2 tablespoons honey
2 tablespoons orange juice
$1/4$ tablespoon olive oil

SALAD
6 cups baby greens (lettuce, arugula, radicchio) washed and dried
$1/2$ cup roasted cashew nuts, coarsely chopped

DRESSING
1 In a mortar, pound together salt, pepper, and ginger to make a paste. Add the honey and whisk together with orange juice and olive oil.

SALAD
2 In a large serving bowl, toss the greens with $1/2$ of the dressing. Sprinkle with the cashew nuts and pour the remaining dressing over the top.

Tropical Salad

SERVES 4

VINAIGRETTE
4 teaspoons salt
2 teaspoons black pepper
2 tablespoons balsamic vinegar
$1/4$ cup olive oil

SALAD
1 passion fruit
3 cups French baby lettuce, washed and dried
1 cup watercress, washed and dried
2 teaspoons salt
1 cup sliced star fruit, persimmons, or mango
2 tablespoons grated Brazil nuts

VINAIGRETTE
1 In a small bowl combine salt, black pepper, and balsamic vinegar. Whisk in the olive oil until it emulsifies. Reserve.

SALAD
2 Cut the passion fruit in half. Place the pulp, including the seeds, in a strainer and press with a spoon. Collect the juice in a small bowl and reserve. Note: You may use bottled passion fruit juice, but the juice of the fresh fruit is better.

3 In a large bowl, mix the greens. Sprinkle salt and $1/2$ of the passion fruit juice on the greens and toss gently.

4 Toss the salad with $1/2$ of the salad dressing.

5 In a large shallow bowl or on individual plates, place a few teaspoons of the passion fruit juice and the vinaigrette in the center of the plate. Arrange the salad in the center of the bowl and arrange the sliced fruit around the salad in a decorative pattern.

6 Sprinkle the grated Brazil nuts around the salad and top with the remaining vinaigrette.

Okra Tomato Salad

SERVES 6

3 cups medium to small okra
4 cups water
4$\frac{1}{2}$ teaspoons salt, divided
2 tablespoons vinegar
3 ripe tomatoes
$\frac{1}{2}$ teaspoon sugar
Black pepper to taste
2 tablespoons balsamic vinegar
3 tablespoons olive oil
$\frac{1}{4}$ cup toasted sesame seeds

1 Clean the okra with a paper towel and set aside. In a large saucepan, bring water, 1$\frac{1}{2}$ teaspoons salt, and vinegar to a boil. Blanch $\frac{1}{2}$ of the okra for 3 minutes; strain, and immerse in a bowl with ice and water. Strain well and set aside. Do remaining batch in same water.

2 Quarter the tomatoes. Seed and remove the center parts. Cut the tomatoes lengthwise into 8 pieces, similar to the size of the okra. You should have about 1$\frac{1}{2}$ cups.

3 Place the cut tomatoes in a strainer and sprinkle with 2 teaspoons salt. Let drain for 15 minutes.

4 In a small bowl, place 1 teaspoon salt, sugar, and black pepper. Whisk in the balsamic vinegar and olive oil.

5 Toss the okra with the tomatoes and $\frac{2}{3}$ of the dressing. Spread the rest of the dressing in the center of a decorative plate. Make a mound with the vegetables and sprinkle with the toasted sesame seeds.

Vatapá Fish Chowder

SERVES 8

4 pounds medium-size shrimp
2 cups water
6 pounds filet of hake, king fish, or
  red snapper
Juice of 2 limes
10 teaspoons salt, divided
6 teaspoons black pepper, divided
1 loaf white bread
2 cups milk
4 tablespoons vegetable oil
2 cups diced onion
5 garlic cloves, peeled and finely
  chopped
8 tomatoes, peeled, seeded, cored,
  and diced
3 cups coconut milk
4 tablespoons palm oil
1/2 cup peanuts, coarsely ground

1 Peel the shrimp and reserve the shells. Wash the shells, place them in a medium-size saucepan with water, and boil for 10 minutes. Drain and reserve the liquid; discard the shells.

2 Devein the shrimp and wash them thoroughly. Refrigerate.

3 Preheat the oven to 275 degrees F.

4 Place the fish filets side by side on an ovenproof dish and season with lime juice, 4 teaspoons salt, and 3 teaspoons pepper.

5 Bake fish for 10 minutes, remove from oven, and reserve.

6 Cut off the bread crusts and discard. Tear the bread slices into 6 pieces and place them in a large bowl.

7 In a medium-size saucepan, warm the milk with 3 teaspoons salt and 2 teaspoons pepper; pour over the bread pieces. Add the shrimp broth to the bowl and let the bread soak for 15 minutes.

8 In a large pot, warm the vegetable oil and sauté the onions for 3 minutes or until they become soft. Add the garlic, 3 teaspoons salt, and 1 teaspoon pepper and cook for a couple of minutes. Add the tomatoes, stir gently to mix all the ingredients, and simmer for 3 minutes more. Add the soaked bread and mix everything well, making sure your spoon scrapes the bottom of the pot. When it starts bubbling, add the coconut milk and gently fold in with circular movements. Boil for 3 minutes and then lower the heat. Add the palm oil and cook over low heat for 10 more minutes.

9 Add the shrimp, folding in gently with large strokes. Keep checking the bottom of the pan to keep the vatapá from sticking.

10 Finally fold in the baked fish and cook for 5 more minutes.

11 Serve the vatapá with white rice or acaçá. Sprinkle with peanuts.

Tereza's Bobó

SERVES 6

BOBÓ STOCK

2 pounds fish heads and tails, washed
8 cups cold water
$1/2$ pound celery stalk, washed, peeled, and cut into large pieces
2 carrots, washed and quartered
1 medium-size onion, peeled and quartered
5 garlic cloves
2 tablespoons shrimp powder or extract (available in Latin American stores)

BOBÓ CREAM

2 pounds manioc
3 cups water
8 teaspoons salt, divided
1 pound large-size shrimp
$1^{1}/3$ cups palm oil, divided
1 pound plantains
1 teaspoon olive oil
3 tomatoes, washed, seeded, cored, and diced
4 garlic cloves, peeled and chopped
1 cup coarsely chopped coriander
1 cup coarsely chopped scallion
2 cups Bobó stock
1 cup coconut milk
Pepper to taste

STOCK

1 In a stockpot, bring the fish heads and tails to boil with water, celery, carrots, onion, and garlic. Lower the heat and let simmer gently for 20 minutes. Using a spoon, remove the foam as it comes to the surface. Strain the liquid, discarding the solids. Bring the stock back to the stockpot, add the shrimp extract, and let it reduce to half. Reserve.

CREAM

2 Peel the manioc, cut in large pieces, and reserve in a bowl with cold water. Place half of the manioc pieces in a large saucepan with just enough water to cover. Add 6 teaspoons salt and bring to boil. Cook the manioc for 20 minutes or until the manioc is soft. Place it in a bowl of ice water. Proceed in the same way with the remaining half of the manioc.

3 Drain the cooked manioc and reserve.

4 Using a meat grinder, grind the manioc twice. Keep it warm and reserve. (Do not use a blender or food processor.)

5 Peel, devein, and wash the shrimp. Reserve and keep cold.

6 In a skillet, warm 1 cup palm oil and pan-sear the shrimp. Keep them warm and reserve.

7 Preheat the oven to 275 degrees F and bake the plantains for 15 minutes or until the skins break. Peel the plantains and reserve.

8 In a large saucepan, warm the olive oil. Add the manioc, plantains, tomato, garlic, coriander, and scallions. Add the Bobó Stock and 2 teaspoons salt and cook for 20 minutes, stirring a couple of times.

9 Gently fold in the shrimp. Add the coconut milk, cook for 3 minutes, and then add $1/3$ cup palm oil. Stir gently to mix all the ingredients. Check the salt and pepper and add more if necessary. Let simmer for 5 more minutes. Serve at once with white rice and hot pepper sauce on the side.

Fish Paupiette with Crabmeat, Brazilian-Style

SERVES 6

- 2 large red bell peppers
- 1 yellow bell pepper
- 1/4 cup vegetable oil
- 3 medium onions, coarsely chopped
- 5 garlic cloves, coarsely chopped
- 1/2 cup chopped cilantro
- 1 pound tomatoes, peeled, seeded, and cut in large pieces or 1 (16-ounce) can tomatoes
- 2 cups fish stock
- 10 teaspoons salt, divided, plus some to taste
- 4 teaspoons pepper
- 1 bay leaf
- 2 egg whites
- 10 ounces crabmeat
- 1/4 cup heavy cream
- 1 teaspoon cayenne pepper
- 3 cups water
- 6 whole scallions, plus scallion tips for decoration
- 1 cup roasted peanuts
- 6 filets of hake, yellow tile, or king fish
- 1 1/2 cups unsweetened coconut milk
- 5 cups Rice with Dendê Béchamel Sauce (page 99)

1 Preheat oven to 400 degrees F. Place the bell peppers on a baking sheet and bake them for 1 hour. When they are finished baking, place them in a covered pan to cool. When they are cool enough to handle, peel the peppers, discard the seeds, and cut them in large squares. Reserve.

2 In a medium-size, heavy-bottom saucepan, heat the oil and sauté the onions for 3 minutes or until soft. Add the garlic, stir well, and then add the chopped cilantro. After 2 minutes, add the tomatoes, stirring well. Add the baked bell peppers and simmer for 15 minutes more. Add the fish stock, 6 teaspoons salt, pepper, and the bay leaf; cover the pan, simmering gently for 30 minutes.

3 Remove from heat, discard the bay leaf, and let cool. Purée the cooled mixture in a food processor or blender until it is smooth and uniform. Reserve.

FILLING

4 Lightly whisk the egg whites and combine with the crabmeat. Add the cream and season with 1 teaspoon salt and cayenne pepper. Reserve.

5 In a small saucepan, bring water to a boil. Place cold water with ice in a bowl. Immerse 1 scallion at a time in the boiling water for 1 minute. Use tongs or a large fork to remove the scallion from the pan. Immerse in the ice water for 3 minutes or until it cools completely. Press along the scallion with your fingers to remove the excess water. Place it flat on parchment paper and reserve.

6 Coarsely grind the roasted peanuts in a food processor or blender.

7 Gently pound the fish filets to flatten them. Place 1 scallion vertically on the counter. Place 1 filet on top of the scallion. Rub the filet with salt and place 2 tablespoons of the crab filling in the center of the filet. Roll the filet firmly, but without pressing, making sure the opening stays at the bottom. Tie the paupiettes gently with the scallions and reserve. Prepare the remaining filets the same way.

8 In a large skillet, heat the vegetable purée over medium-high heat. When it is simmering, add the coconut milk, stirring and cooking for 3 minutes.

9 Distribute the paupiettes around the skillet and cover with parchment paper. (Do not use a lid.) Make sure the paupiettes are immersed in the sauce. Poach the paupiettes for 20 minutes over medium heat.

10 To serve, place 1/2 cup of the Rice with Béchamel Sauce in the center of a plate, forming a 5-inch circle. Place one paupiette on top of the rice. Pour the vegetable purée around the rice and sprinkle with ground peanuts. Garnish with scallion tips.

11 Or, you may pour 1/2 of the sauce on a 2-inch-deep platter and arrange the paupiettes around it. Garnish with scallion tips. Serve the rest of the sauce in a jar and the roasted peanuts in a small bowl. In a serving bowl, place the rice mixed with the palm oil béchamel. Serve at once with hot pepper sauce.

Seafood Moqueca Paraíso Tropical

SERVES 8

SEAFOOD

$1/2$ pound mussels, washed and
  debearded
2–3 pounds fish filets (hake, king
  fish, monk fish, tile fish)
$1/2$ pound shrimp, peeled and
  deveined
$1/2$ pound sea scallops, washed
Juice of 2 limes
12 teaspoons salt, divided
8 teaspoons pepper

MOQUECA

1 cup coconut milk
1 fresh green coconut or 2 cups
  bottled coconut juice
2 cups peeled and julienned
  onions
3 large red bell peppers, cored,
  seeded, and cut in julienne
1 pound tomatoes, peeled, and
  seeded, and cut in julienne or 1
  (16-ounce) can tomatoes
$1/2$ cup coarsely chopped cilantro
$1/2$ cup coarsely chopped parsley
$1/2$ cup coarsely chopped scallions
$1/4$ cup vegetable oil
$1/4$ cup palm oil
$1/4$ cup finely chopped onion
6 garlic cloves, finely chopped
$1/2$ cup finely chopped cilantro,
  divided
1 bay leaf, crumbled
Pepper to taste
3 cups fish stock, divided
3 tablespoons palm oil, preheated
  in the microwave for 1 minute
  or in boiling water for
  3 minutes

SEAFOOD

1 Place the mussels on a tray and refrigerate.

2 Place the fish filets, shrimp, and scallops on a deep platter. Sprinkle with lime juice, 6 teaspoons salt, and 4 teaspoons pepper, and marinate for $1/2$ hour. Strain before using.

MOQUECA

3 Cook and serve the moqueca in the same pan. Use an earthenware or braiser pan.

4 If you are using a fresh green coconut, make a hole with a sharp knife. Pour the coconut water into a container and reserve. (If you are not using immediately, keep refrigerated.) Open the coconut in half and scoop out all the white pulp with a spoon and place in a bowl. Blend the juice with the pulp and reserve.

5 If using bottled coconut juice, whisk it with the coconut milk. Reserve.

6 In a large bowl, toss the onions, bell peppers, tomatoes, and the coarsely chopped cilantro, parsley, and scallions. Reserve.

7 In a large pan or braiser, heat the vegetable oil with the palm oil and sauté the chopped onion for 2 minutes; add the garlic and $1/3$ of the finely chopped cilantro and stir well. Add the bay leaf, season with 6 teaspoons salt and 4 teaspoons pepper, and add 1 cup of the fish stock. Let simmer for 5 minutes. Remove pan from heat and let cool for 10 minutes.

8 Make layers, alternating the vegetables and herbs with the fish, shrimp, and scallops, ending with the vegetables, mussels, and herbs.

9 Pour the coconut mixture and 1 cup of fish stock around the layers. The liquid should barely cover the fish and vegetables. Cook, covered, over medium-high heat for 15 minutes. Check the seasonings and adjust if necessary. Add preheated palm oil evenly around the pan. Lower the heat and simmer, uncovered, for another 10 minutes. Sprinkle with the remaining cilantro.

10 Serve at once with white rice, Palm Oil Farofa, and Malagueta Hot Pepper Sauce. (pages 100–101.)

Chicken Xim-Xim

5 garlic cloves
10 teaspoons salt, divided
$1/2$ cup vegetable oil
2–3 pounds chicken cut in 8 parts, fat trimmed, washed and patted dry
5 teaspoons pepper
2 medium onions, chopped
1 cup chopped cilantro
1 pound tomatoes, peeled and seeded or 1 (16-ounce) can whole tomatoes, drained, and cut in 4 pieces
2 tablespoons tomato paste
3 teaspoons Tabasco or hot pepper, crushed
3 bay leaves
4 cups water
3 tablespoons flour
1 cup coconut milk
3 tablespoons dendê palm oil
$1/2$ cup cashew nuts, crushed

1 Crush garlic and 2 teaspoons salt together in a mortar. Reserve.

2 In a large heavy pan, heat oil and sear 3 pieces of chicken at a time on both sides until light brown. Remove the chicken from the pan and put in a bowl. Spread 3 teaspoons salt and 2 teaspoons pepper around the seared chicken pieces. Cover and keep warm. Proceed in the same way with the remaining chicken. Use 2 teaspoons salt and 1 teaspoon pepper after searing the last two pieces. Allow the pan to cool for 5 minutes.

3 Reheat the pan and sauté the onions until soft. Add the garlic, and as you stir, scrape the bottom of the pan to collect all the fond left by the searing of the chicken. Cook for 1 minute, mixing all the ingredients. Add 2 teaspoons salt, the cilantro, and tomatoes and cook on medium heat for 3 minutes. Add the tomato paste and the Tabasco or hot pepper sauce and cook for 3–4 more minutes.

4 Place browned chicken pieces and their juices in the pan, making sure that all the pieces are coated with the sauce. Add the bay leaves and just enough cold water to cover the chicken. Add the rest of the salt, cover the pan, and cook the chicken slowly for 1 hour. Let cool for 15 minutes. Strain the chicken, reserving the liquid, and then strain the liquid. Place the chicken in a shallow tray and, using a fork and knife, separate the meat from the bones. Discard the bones. Finely shred the meat using 2 forks.

5 Sprinkle the shredded pieces of chicken with flour, mixing thoroughly to coat all the shredded chicken.

6 Place the chicken back in the pan and add the cooking liquid, stirring gently. Let it simmer, uncovered, for 5 minutes over medium heat. Gently fold in the coconut milk and simmer for 5 minutes.

7 Fifteen minutes before serving, warm the palm oil for 2 minutes in the microwave or 5 minutes in a double bath. Add the palm oil to the chicken xim-xim and cook for 5 minutes, stirring gently.

8 Sprinkle with crushed cashew nuts and serve with rice or Acaçá (page 99).

Rice with Dendê Béchamel Sauce

SERVES 6

4 tablespoons butter
1¹/₂ teaspoons vegetable oil
4 tablespoons flour
2 cups milk
Salt and pepper to taste
3 tablespoons dendê palm oil
4 cups hot cooked rice

1 In a small heavy saucepan, melt the butter with the vegetable oil until it foams. Add the flour at once and stir to form a roux. Slowly pour in the milk and whisk, beating vigorously to prevent lumps. Keep whisking for about 5 minutes. Season with salt and pepper. Fold in the palm oil, simmering for 4 minutes.

2 Mix the béchamel with the rice.

Acaçá (Steamed Rice Flour Polenta)

SERVES 6

4 tablespoons olive oil
2¹/₂ cups coconut milk
2 cups milk
Salt and pepper to taste
3 cups rice flour
1 cup heavy cream
2 tablespoons vegetable oil

1 In a large saucepan, mix together the olive oil, coconut milk, milk, salt, and pepper and bring to a boil over high heat. Reduce the heat to medium and whisk in the rice flour a little at a time, stirring constantly until the mixture is smooth and thick (about 8 minutes). Gradually add the cream and mix.

2 Coat a flat serving dish lightly with 1 tablespoon oil. Pour the acaçá into the pan and, using a spatula, press it flat. Spread 1 tablespoon oil around it. Keep covered at room temperature until ready to serve. Cut acaçá into 3-inch circles and serve as a side dish.

Cosme and Damião Caruru

SERVES 6

1 pound okra, washed and dried, both ends trimmed
4 cups fish or vegetable broth, divided
$^1/_3$ cup palm oil
$^1/_2$ cup finely chopped onion
$^1/_4$ cup finely processed smoked shrimp
$^1/_8$ cup smoked shrimp, whole
1 teaspoon finely chopped fresh ginger
$^1/_4$ cup ground unsalted cashew nuts
$^1/_8$ cup ground unsalted peanuts
Salt and pepper to taste
$1^1/_2$ cups coconut milk

1 Cut the okra in half and set aside.

2 Heat the fish or vegetable broth and keep hot.

3 In a medium-size saucepan, heat the palm oil and sauté the onion for 3 minutes. Add both processed and whole shrimp and stir together. Add the okra, ginger, cashew nuts, and peanuts. Season with salt and pepper.

4 Add 1 cup of the fish or vegetable broth and stir. Keep adding more broth as needed until the okra is cooked. Finally, add the coconut milk and simmer for 10 minutes.

5 The caruru can be served alone or with vatapá.

Malagueta Hot Pepper Sauce

YIELDS 1 CUP

$^1/_4$ cup preserved malagueta pepper or any preserved chili
4 tablespoons finely chopped onion
6 tablespoons lime juice
3 tablespoons olive oil

1 In a bowl or mortar, crush the peppers with the onion and lime juice to make a paste. Add the olive oil and whisk.

2 Place in a covered jar and keep refrigerated.

Milk Pirão

SERVES 4

2 cups milk
2 cups manioc flour
Salt to taste
1 tablespoon butter
Parsley and scallions for garnish

1 In a medium-size saucepan, add the milk and the manioc flour and mix well. Simmer on low heat for 5 minutes, whisking to prevent lumps. Season with salt; add the butter just before serving. Place in a serving bowl decorated with parsley and sliced scallions.

2 Serve as a side dish with fish, poultry, or beef.

Palm Oil Farofa

SERVES 6

1 tablespoon vegetable oil
2 tablespoons palm oil
1 tablespoon finely chopped garlic
3 cups manioc flour
Salt and pepper to taste

1 In a heavy skillet, heat the vegetable oil and the palm oil over medium heat. Sauté the garlic until soft. Slowly sift the manioc flour through your fingers into the center of the skillet. Stir in a circular motion while you are adding the flour to mix the ingredients well. (During this process, the manioc is cooking and toasting.) It should take 3 to 5 minutes.

2 Season with salt and pepper. Serve at once as a side dish.

Mango Galette

SERVES 6

9 tablespoons chilled unsalted butter
2 cups all-purpose flour
Pinch of salt
$1/2$ cup ice water, divided
2 mangoes, ripe but firm
2 tablespoons heavy cream
4 tablespoons sugar
2 tablespoons butter
$1^1/2$ teaspoons lime zest
Sprig of mint or flowers

1 Cut the butter into small cubes and place in the freezer for 10 minutes. In a large bowl, mix the flour with the salt. Place the chilled butter in the bowl, and with the tips of your fingers, press the flour with the butter, forming crumbs. Make a small hole in the center of the mixture and pour 4 tablespoons ice water into it. Gently mix the water with the flour and butter mixture by moving your fingers like the wings of a butterfly. The flour will flow through your fingers and it will absorb the water (the result should not be too wet). Proceed in the same way until no dry flour is left on the bottom of the bowl.

2 Place the dough on a cold counter.

3 With the palm of one hand, smash the dough to combine the flour and the butter. Repeat it in order to create a marbled texture. Wrap the dough in plastic wrap and place in the refrigerator for 30 minutes.

4 Remove the dough from the refrigerator. Sprinkle flour over a cold counter and start flattening the dough slowly by pushing down with the rolling pin to make indents. Turn the dough 90 degrees and proceed in the same way until the dough is $1/2$ inch wide. Add more flour to the counter and the rolling pin as needed. Working rapidly with the rolling pin, flatten the dough, making sure not to press too hard. Turn the dough clockwise 45 degrees each time and proceed in the same way. You should have a circle 12 inches wide and $1/2$ inch thick.

5 Cover a cookie sheet with parchment paper and place the circle on it. Refrigerate for 30 minutes.

6 Peel the mangoes and cut in $\frac{1}{3}$-inch slices. Reserve.

7 Preheat the oven to 400 degrees F. Remove the dough from the refrigerator. Distribute the mango slices starting from the center, creating rows in a decorative pattern. Stop placing the mango slices 2 inches before the edges of the dough. Fold the edges gently over the fruit. Make creases on the dough as you fold. Refrigerate the galette if not baking immediately.

8 Just before baking the galette, brush the dough evenly with cream and sprinkle with 2 tablespoons sugar. Distribute small dollops of butter around the fruit, sprinkle with lime zest, and bake for 30 minutes in the lower section of the oven. Lower the heat to 325 degrees F and move the cookie sheet to the mid-oven rack. Bake for another 10–15 minutes until the fruit is slightly golden.

9 Remove from the oven and cool for 10 minutes. Slide the galette onto a serving platter and sprinkle with the remaining 2 tablespoons sugar around the mango.

10 Garnish with mint leaves or flowers.

Quindim (Coconut Custard, Bahía Way)

SERVES 8

1 pound plus $1/3$ cup sugar, divided
2 cups water
2 tablespoons butter, plus more for coating pan
12 egg yolks
$2^{1}/_{2}$ cups grated coconut*
2 tablespoons raisins

* Do not use commercially packaged sweetened coconut. However, you may use frozen grated coconut.

1 Preheat the oven to 375 degrees F.

2 Place 1 pound sugar and water in a saucepan and slowly simmer over low heat. Do not stir the mixture but rather let it sit and cook until you obtain a thick syrup. (Use a dessert fork and lift some of the syrup: you should see very heavy drops falling from the tines of the fork.) Add 2 tablespoons butter to the syrup and let it cool completely.

3 Pass the egg yolks through a sieve or strainer. When the syrup is cold, add the egg yolks to the syrup and mix gently. Fold in the coconut until it is totally mixed. Let rest for 2 hours.

4 Coat a springform pan with butter and sprinkle with $1/3$ cup sugar. Shake well to eliminate the excess.

5 Pour the batter into the pan and bake in a double bath for 1 hour. Let cool and then turn it over onto a serving plate.

6 Distribute the raisins evenly around the top of the quindim.

Regal Banana

SERVES 6

6 bananas
1 tablespoon lime juice
2 cups plus 6 tablespoons sugar, divided
$1/2$ cup water
2 tablespoons unsalted butter, plus more for coating pan
4 eggs, separated
$2^1/4$ cups whole milk, divided
1 tablespoon cornmeal (Maizena)
4 pieces lime rind (green only)

1 Peel bananas and cut them into $1^1/2$-inch slices. Sprinkle with lime juice and reserve.

2 **For the caramel:** In a medium-size heavy saucepan, bring 2 cups sugar and water to a low simmer until it becomes a light caramel color. Turn off the heat and add the butter. Allow it to melt and shake the saucepan a couple of times to mix the caramel with the butter. Place the bananas in the saucepan and return to the stove. When it is warm, turn off the heat and reserve.

3 **For the cream:** Whisk the egg yolks until they foam. Add 2 tablespoons sugar and whisk until the mixture becomes white. Reserve.

4 In a small bowl, mix 1 tablespoon milk with the cornmeal. Set aside.

5 In a medium-size saucepan, bring 2 cups milk and the lime rind to a boil. Lower the heat and simmer for 5 minutes. Remove and discard the lime rind.

6 Add 1 tablespoon milk to the beaten egg yolks and whisk well. Slowly pour the beaten eggs over the milk in the saucepan as you whisk rapidly. Finally, add the cornmeal-milk mixture to the saucepan, whisking for 4–5 minutes more. Remove from the heat and reserve.

7 **For the meringue:** Beat the egg whites to a stiff peak. Add 4 tablespoons sugar and beat lightly. Reserve.

8 Preheat the oven to 325 degrees F.

9 Coat a 2-inch-deep, ceramic, ovenproof rectangular pan with butter.

10 Distribute the caramelized bananas evenly on the bottom of the plate. Pour the cream gently over the bananas, spreading with a spoon to cover them completely. Using a spatula, spread the meringue over the cream and use a fork to make decorative swirls.

11 Bake for 15 minutes or until the meringue is golden. Let it cool and serve at room temperature, or refrigerate before serving.

Tapioca Muffins

1 cup tapioca flour
1/2 cup plus 3 tablespoons butter, divided
1 1/3 cup sugar plus 2 tablespoons, divided
3/4 cup flour
4 eggs
1 1/3 cup coconut milk
1/2 cup freshly grated coconut
1/2 cup grated parmegiano cheese
1 teaspoon baking powder

1 In a food processor or blender, beat the tapioca for 2 minutes, pulsing the tapioca 8–10 times to make the grains of the tapioca thinner. Reserve.

2 In a large bowl, place 1/2 cup and 1 tablespoon butter and 1 1/3 cups sugar. Beat well until it becomes a cream. You may do it by hand or with an electric beater. In a medium bowl, combine both flours and reserve.

3 Add the eggs one at a time to the cream and keep beating until the batter becomes homogeneous. Add the combined flours alternating with the coconut milk and keep beating until all the ingredients are well mixed.

4 Add the grated coconut, cheese, and baking powder and beat for 2–3 minutes more. Let it rest.

5 Preheat the oven to 300 F.

6 Coat 8 ramekins with 2 tablespoons softened butter and sprinkle with 2 tablespoons sugar. Distribute the batter in the ramekins and bake for 40 minutes. Let it cool.

7 Serve it topped with warm butter for breakfast or as a dessert with strawberries and cream.

The Cooking of Minas Gerais

The news about gold and precious stones found in the interior of Brazil in the late 1600s, precipitated an important change in the direction of the country.

Thousands of people joined organized groups who followed the course of treacherous rivers as they fought their way through the coastal mountains and dense tropical forests to seek their fortune somewhere inland.

People from all corners of life—young and old, rich and poor, nobles and gentlemen who had been living close to the coast—left behind everything they had, their families and friends, their homes, and their jobs. The resulting journey proved difficult, and people were unprepared for the challenges nature presented them.

Many died of disease, animal attacks, and, most of all, hunger. Their supply of food wasn't sufficient, and long distances made it impossible for new provisions to reach the adventurers. Learning about their new environment became essential to their survival. At first, they learned from the Indians to eat insects, wood worms, and roots. The Indians ate a particular ant called *içá*, a delicacy for them, which also gained some converts among the trekkers. One Portuguese noble-man named Gabriel Soares da Costa wrote regularly to his wife in Portugal about his travels in Brazil, mentioning the *içá* and saying that its taste reminded him of the raisins of Alicante in Spain, a refined and expensive ingredient in Europe.

Interestingly, Africans, Chinese, and the Aztecs of Mexico also ate ants as part of their regular diet. They apparently have a valuable nutrient value of 5 percent protein, and small amounts of fat and minerals.

The pace of the expeditions inland was determined by the seasons. During the period of heavy rains, when it was impossible to cross the torrential rivers and keep marching, the pioneers chose a sheltered place where they could improvise a settlement, often staying as long as six months. They used this time to plant corn, beans, and squash. They frequently harvested the crops before going forward, and they left a small plantation behind in the settlement for those who would come later.

When i was a youngster and living in Minas Gerais, a taste for such "strange" things was neither foreign nor odd to me and some of my five- and six-year-old friends. During the month of October, millions of *tanajuras* (ants) came flying in packs. With our natural childhood exuberance, we chased and caught the tanajuras as we flooded the neighborhood with our enthusiastic voices and laughter. We discarded the heads and wings, but kept the bellies to suck their sweetness. Then, steamed up with energy, we went for more! Decades later, in the '80s, I lived in Mexico City with my husband and daughter. There, I used to go with some Mexican friends to an eighty-year-old downtown restaurant called Don Chon that prepared, among other pre-Hispanic dishes, the ants of my childhood, called *necuazcatl* in the Nahuatl language.

As soon as the rains ceased, the travelers used sickles and large knives to open trails through inhospitable vegetation, and they traveled marshes infested with insects. Yet nothing seemed to discourage them, and they persisted. Those who survived the harshness of the year-long expedition reached the district of Rio das Mortes (Death River) and the Tripuí River in Ouro Preto (Black Gold), where the first signs of gold were discovered.

Black granular nodules were found along local riverbanks and were immediately identified as being among the purest forms of gold deposit. By 1690, expeditions discovered additional deposits of ore, and this caused a proliferation of mine activity. Primitive hamlets developed here and there along these riverbanks as the miners built their shacks.

This ensemble of the mines and their settlements was called Minas Gerais or General Mines. Mining the gold was the most important and sometimes the sole occupation for the majority of the 30,000 people living in Minas Gerais in the early 1700s, including African slaves who had begun to arrive in 1680. At the mine area, there was little interest in farming or time to devote to it.

Convoys carrying all sorts of provisions had to travel for months over thousands of miles from as far as Pernambuco and Bahía in the north and São Paulo in the south and across steep mountains to reach the people living in these small villages. Twice this isolation proved disastrous, culminating in two episodes of famine: one in 1698 and the other in 1713, when people died of hunger, even though they had gold in their pockets and bagfuls in their houses.

With the finding of new deposits of gold, and then diamonds, even more people came to live in the region, particularly noble Portuguese. One such was Dom Pedro de Almeida e Portugal, the Comte of Assumar, who acted as governor of the province and lived in a comfortable residence in Ouro Preto.

He insisted that the residents plant food crops. Besides planting manioc as they had learned to do from the Indians, he got them to plant squash, corn, and beans.

The settlers also took advantage of such marvelous local fruit as the *jabuticaba* that grows without stems, directly on the trunk and branches of the tree.

With the cultivation of corn, mills were built and flour production began. That flour became the basis for many of the traditional dishes of Minas Gerais cuisine. As the supply of food and other goods became more constant, the threat of another episode of famine receded.

The shortage of food that marked this period and the geographic isolation of the region are at the origin of and have become the basis for the cooking in Minas Gerais. The basic ingredients were beans, corn, and manioc, each with its own flour, plus the preserved meats that came from Bahía or São Paulo. The most common dish that miners ate was made in a single pot hanging from a tripod over an open fire. Beans were cooked slowly in water in the pot, and pieces of dried salted meats were added. To eat, they sat around a large straw mat stretched on the ground

with a sack of manioc flour placed in the center as a table. They ate beans on tin plates, helping themselves to generous portions of manioc flour, a resilient food that was filling and nourishing. The meal ended with honey, native fruits, and *aluá,* a kind of brandy made with fermented corn that they drank in squash gourds (called *cuias* by the Indians).

This basic dish, combined with eggs and bacon, gave origin to the *feijão tropeiro* or tropeiro beans, one of many typical and delicious dishes that characterizes the foods of Minas Gerais. (*Tropeiro* means people traveling in caravans.)

In addition to making aluá, corn was used to make a variety of foods. Among these was a type of porridge the Indians called *curau,* and another of the most typical dishes in Minas Gerais: the *angú.* Angú is a soft polenta made with corn flour. It was cooked slowly in unsalted boiling water in large copper pans. Primarily made for the slaves, it soon became everyone's food—a side dish that accommodated all demands. The angú that became indispensable on the miners' table then has remained unchanged and part of everyday meals in all Minas Gerais today.

Occasionally, during the colonial times in Minas, it was possible to find chicken, eggs, and sugar to buy, but at absurdly high prices. Letters written by the Jesuits in 1703, for instance, document that a chicken sold for 4,000 *réis* (the name of the currency then) in Minas Gerais, while it sold for 160 réis in São Paulo close to the coast. Similarly, one pound of sugar sold for 1,200 réis in the mining regions and for 120 réis in São Paulo. Salt, according to those letters, was extremely rare and when found, could cost fifty times more than in the ports! People got most of their salt intake from the salty preserved meats and it was a constant burden to get any extra amount. By the king's decree, the royal monopoly of salt finally ended on May 27, 1795, thus easing the scarcity.

For the next few decades in Minas Gerais, there was an increase in discoveries of gold and diamonds and a corresponding rise in general commercial activity.

Such relative prosperity attracted nobles and emissaries from the court, and, with their arrival, profound changes came to the daily life of the people living in the region. Due to the region's wealth and economic growth, it was of great interest to Portugal. Minas Gerais became the epicenter of colonial politics, and from its prosperity and relative sophistication dawned a spirit of independence and eventually the movements for the independence of Brazil.

Among the most visible changes produced by the arrival of courtiers were those that affected cooking and the table. Prior to the immigrants' arrival, slaves did the cooking, and dishes were simply made with ingredients available locally. The new arrivals used considerable teaching flair to build upon the already available cooking skills and creativity (particularly among the Africans) to improve the meals and to expand the repertoire of recipes. For example, they showed the local cooks how to use corn and manioc flours to make more elaborate savory dishes as well as to bake goods and desserts.

New dishes such as marinated roasted pork loin and whole suckling pig, sausages, baked stuffed quail, and chicken stews with strong Portuguese influence became part of the Brazilian table. The African women in charge of the cooking had learned from the Indians to include some fruits like the native pineapple and bananas, grilled or baked, to accompany meats.

A select group of residents was able to include ingredients that came from Portugal in their cooking. They could use dried fruits such as apricots, prunes, and raisins, as well as spices such as cinnamon, nutmeg, and cloves. If a person had access to these ingredients, it meant that he or she had connections with the court of Portugal or had other important political ties. Those precious ingredients that gave a special touch to the dishes were kept under guarded lock and key and were used only on special occasions when there were important travelers to entertain. In contrast, the valuable gold bars

could have been stacked with neglect in a corner of the house.

The table setting also grew more elaborate and more elegant. The tablecloths were made with linen and laces and were embroidered by hand. Silver and beautiful china from England, India, and Macao were shipped from Europe, along with fine crystal, and brought to the now prosperous villages of Minas Gerais.

There were two reasons for this. First was the new availability, again to a select few, of fine linens and tableware shipped from the continent, and second was a marked increase in the number of occasions that called for their use. Some of these occasions were related to European religious celebrations such as Christmas, the Feast of the Magi, Easter, and the celebrations of saints during the month of June.

Other occasions for elegance were to entertain guests from England, Germany, France, Holland, and elsewhere. Such people might have been attracted by news about the gold and diamonds in Minas Gerais, or they might have been historians, botanists, or other scientists who traveled to the region to see its marvels with their own eyes. The latter described in great detail the land and daily life of the population living in that province. Their observations were invaluable! They tell us, for instance, about dining with important visitors.

Typically, before dinner, well-dressed men stood on the veranda drinking Porto, talking about the weather, mining activities,

Exterior and portal
of Nossa Senhora
do Rosário dos
Pretos in Ouro
Preto.

agriculture, court politics, and the latest news from Bahía, São Paulo, and Europe. The women, who dressed elegantly in European-style clothes and wore gold necklaces, stayed inside in the parlor.

At dinner it was the custom for the ladies to sit on one side of the table with the men on the other; the married women were always opposite their husbands. The owner of the house served each guest from the head of the table, passing the plates around. He also poured the wine, but the ladies sipped it only during the toasts, with their lips barely touching the glasses.

At the center of the elegant table lay a great number of fragrant dishes placed there by female servants all dressed in impeccable white. The visitors were usually astonished at the variety and abundance of the food before them. It often included *pururuca*, whole baked suckling piglet with its skin crispy and golden and the meat falling off the bones; moist pork loin roast served with a succulent sauce; whole quails stuffed with corn flour and raisins; stewed chicken cooked slowly with okra; and local herbs and spices in a rich sauce made with *urucum* (a native spice that turns the sauce a vivid red-orange). There were usually two or three types of delicious cooked bean dishes plus savory squash, the indispensable angú, and sautéed collard greens cut paper-thin.

Manioc or corn flour (a replacement for bread) was customarily placed in the center of the table on an attractive platter or bowl.

It was common for the locals to eat with their fingers as well as with a fork and knife.

Etiquette, however, advised the use of only three fingers—the thumb, index, and middle fingers. During the feast, servants brought silver bowls with scented water and little linen towels with which guests cleaned their fingers.

Desserts were sumptuous, presented in elegant crystal bowls placed in the center of the table. At one of these dinners, a guest noted twenty-nine desserts: native fruits preserved in thick syrup, puddings made with dried fruits and bread, rich egg custards, and crèmes of caramelized milk and cheeses paired with desserts. If complimented by the guests, the lady of the house proudly made it clear that house slaves had prepared all the dishes.

After dinner the guests were served English black tea, coffee, or tisane made with regional herbs or orange leaves. This was followed by tobacco for the men. On some occasions, a young woman played the piano or the balalaika, with everybody singing the chorus of familiar tunes.

I have the most vivid memories of the wild beauty of the mountains, the azure sky of Minas Gerais,

and the feeling of the fresh air in my face that all come back when I recall horseback riding with my parents, brothers, and cousins.

One such journey started at five o'clock in the morning. The night before, we children gathered a few clothes, boots, hats, and a packet with snacks and water. Contrary to other evenings, we jumped in bed without argument and fell asleep immediately. After a good breakfast consisting of fruit, hot milk with honey, and *pão queijo* (cheese bread), we left the farm where we spent our winter vacations to start our two-day voyage to one of the highest points in the region, which one could reach only by horseback. For us children, it was the stop we made around lunchtime at an impressive nineteenth-century farm that belonged to our host's friends . . . and what a lunch was waiting for us!

It was obvious that our visit was an important occasion, as shown by the detailed preparation everybody had gone through. The house was spotless, the wood furniture and floor were shining. Large flower and colorful fruit arrangements gave the final touch to the special encounter.

After having gone through a long line of people whom we greeted politely, we were free to go with our host's children, who took us running to the kitchen for a first round of fresh juice and incredible fried cookies made with *polvilho* (manioc starch). Talking all at once, they filled us in on the latest news that had happened the year before: calves

were born, a chicken laid one egg with two or three egg yolks(!), the house dog scared a wolf passing by, and of course, the employees of the farm saw, for sure, the headless she-mule one dark night . . . I grabbed another cookie just to quiet my fears. Just before going to the stable to see the new horse, I caught a quick glimpse of the table in the dining room and my eyes widened in disbelief. The table was dressed by a lovely embroidered tablecloth and was piled high with scrumptious-looking dishes. Just behind the table on the mantel were endless desserts!

Some fifteen dishes were on the table and among those were pork loin roast, chicken civet, freshwater fish, a roast, bean dishes, rice, okra, pumpkin, collard greens, farofas, grilled bananas, lots of green salads, and desserts! A range of tropical fruit in shiny syrup, doce de leite, guava paste, custards, and regal banana (made specially for my father), were all presented in elegant glass bowls and white china trays.

Tiny little cups of coffee and shots of the farm's cachaça were served on the large veranda with little cookies that melted in our mouths, announcing the beginning of the long goodbye, Brazilian way.

We parted. I looked back, waving my hand until the next curve suddenly swallowed it all up—but not my souvenirs.

Those visits evoked the way it used to happen in Minas Gerais in the eighteenth century, when visitors came from far away and experienced the traditional hospitality of Minas Gerais.

the recipes of minas gerais

APPETIZERS AND SALADS
Collard Greens Bambá Soup
Green Salad with Pumpkin Seeds and Canastra Cheese
Manioc Croutons
Cheese Rolls, Minas Gerais–Style
Cornmeal Dumplings
Pumpkin Soufflé
Collard Greens Mineira Salad
Salad with Chayote and Pumpkin

MAIN COURSES
Baked Fish, Pirapora-Style
Chicken Stew with Okra
Pork Roast, Vila Rica–Style
Cow in Muddy Sauce

SIDE DISHES
Beans from Minas
Flake Cornmeal Farofa
Glazed Baked Sweet Potatoes
Black Bean Tutu

DESSERTS
Pineapple, Colonial-Style
Corn Crème Brûlée
White Egg and Prune Pudding
Doce de Leite Parfait with Candied Banana

Collard Greens Bambá Soup

SERVES 6

3 cups collard greens (about
  4 bunches), divided
1/2 pound Portuguese-style
  sausage
1 tablespoon plus 1 cup vegetable
  oil, divided
1 cup cornmeal
5 cups chicken broth
5 teaspoons salt

1 Place a collard green leaf on a flat surface and, using a paring knife, make two parallel lengthwise cuts to remove the core. Proceed in the same way with the remaining leaves.

2 Place 6 leaves on top of one another and roll into a small, tight cylinder (like a cigar). Hold this roll against the cutting board so that just a half inch or so shows. Slice down on this end to make the thinnest cut you can manage (perhaps a sixteenth of an inch). Using a really sharp knife, thinly cut the entire roll. Spread out the now-shredded collard greens over a tray and cover with a damp kitchen towel. Proceed the same way with the remaining leaves. Set aside 1 cup cut collard greens for garnish.

3 Slice the sausages in 1/2-inch slices. In a heavy skillet, heat 1 tablespoon oil and sear the sausage slices until they are slightly grilled. Keep them covered and warm.

4 To make the soup, place the cornmeal in a heavy skillet and roast it over medium-high heat, mixing constantly with a spatula to prevent the cornmeal from becoming brown. Pour the cornmeal into a stockpot and let it cool for a couple of minutes.

5 Slowly add the chicken broth to the cornmeal and whisk it to prevent any lumps. Gently boil the soup for 10 minutes, stirring a couple of times. Raise the heat, add the salt and collard greens, and simmer for another 5 minutes.

6 Add the grilled sausages with their juices to the stockpot and stir gently. Cook for 10 more minutes. Keep it warm and covered.

7 In a small skillet, heat 1 cup oil and fry the remaining collard greens for 30 seconds. Strain and set aside.

8 Serve the soup at once, topped with the crispy collard greens.

Green Salad with Pumpkin Seeds and Canastra Cheese

SERVES 6

DRESSING

4 teaspoons salt
2 teaspoons pepper
4 teaspoons raspberry or straw-
  berry jam
3 tablespoons fruity vinegar of
  your choice
5 tablespoons olive oil

SALAD

4 cups lettuce, washed and dried
1 cup watercress
$1/2$ cup pumpkin seeds, roasted
$1/2$ cup Canastra cheese* slivers or
  Pecorino cheese
6 cheese rolls (optional, page 126)

* Canastra cheese is from the
  mountains of Minas Gerais.

DRESSING

1 Combine salt, pepper, and jam in a small bowl. Whisk in the vinegar and the olive oil.

SALAD

2 Mix the greens in a large bowl. Toss the salad with half the dressing.

3 On individual plates, place a few drops of the dressing in the center and make a pile with the greens. Distribute the pumpkin seeds and 2 or 3 cheese slivers around the greens.

4 If using cheese rolls, cut them in fourths and place them on the edge of the plate.

5 Sprinkle 2–3 teaspoons dressing around the greens.

Manioc Croutons

YIELDS 1$^1/_2$ CUPS

4 cups water
10 teaspoons salt, divided
2 cups manioc, peeled and diced
  into $1/4$-inch cubes
3 cups vegetable oil

1 Bring the water and 8 teaspoons salt to a boil and cook the manioc for 3 minutes. Immerse in a bowl with ice water. Drain and pat dry. Reserve.

2 Heat oil in a medium-size sauce-pan; when the oil is very hot but not smoking, fry $1/4$ cup of manioc cubes until golden.

3 With a slotted spoon, remove the manioc croutons and place them in a bowl. Cover them with a paper towel to absorb the excess oil. Sprinkle with salt.

4 Repeat the same process with the remaining manioc.

Cheese Rolls, Minas Gerais-Style

YIELDS 50

1 pound sour polvilho (manioc starch)

1 pound sweet polvilho (manioc starch)

2^1/$_2$ cups milk, divided (reserve ^{1}/$_2$ cup for kneading the dough)

2 tablespoons butter

2 tablespoons salt

5 eggs

^{1}/$_4$ pound grated feta cheese*

^{1}/$_2$ pound grated Parmigiano cheese*

1^1/$_2$ teaspoons vegetable oil

*The ideal cheese is an aged "Mineiro cheese" type.

1 Combine both polvilhos in a large bowl. Boil 2 cups milk with the butter and salt and pour over the polvilhos at once.

2 Working with two forks, mix the flour and the milk to break up the lumps. When the dough is cool enough to touch with your fingers, begin kneading the dough with both hands. Add one egg and knead the dough until the egg is incorporated into the mixture. Add the remaining eggs, kneading each time. If, at this point, the dough feels hard and dry, slowly add more milk as you keep kneading it. (The dough at this point is still not completely homogeneous.)

3 Add the cheeses and gently knead in. The dough should now be smooth and soft.

4 Let it rest for 20 minutes covered with a wet kitchen towel.

5 Preheat the oven to 400 degrees F. Coat a cookie sheet lightly with oil or cover with parchment paper.

6 Coat your hands with a dash of oil or butter. Take one tablespoon of the dough in your hands and roll the dough, making strawberry-size balls. If you prefer, work with two dessert spoons. Place the balls on the cookie sheet, leaving ^{1}/$_2$ inch between them. Bake for 15 minutes. Lower the heat to 325 degrees F and bake for another 10 minutes or until golden. Serve warm. You may also freeze the cheese balls for later baking and use.

Cornmeal Dumplings

YIELDS 40

2 tablespoons salt
1 bay leaf
4 garlic cloves
1¼ cup scallions, cut into fourths, divided
6 cups water, divided
2 medium onions, quartered, divided
4¼ cups whole cornmeal, divided
2 tablespoons plus 4 cups vegetable oil, divided
1 chili, seeded
1¼ pounds ground meat
Salt and pepper to taste

1 Place salt, bay leaf, garlic, and ¾ of the scallions in a mortar and pound together until it becomes a thick paste.

2 In a blender or food processor, mix 2 cups water, ¾ of the onions, and the scallion mixture. Add 2 cups cornmeal and blend again for a couple of minutes.

3 In a large saucepan, bring 4 cups of water to a complete boil. Pour in the cornmeal batter slowly and beat vigorously with a wooden spoon to prevent lumps from forming.

4 When the consistency is creamy, cover the pan and cook the batter for one hour on low heat.

5 Add the remaining cornmeal to the saucepan and mix well; cook for another 10 minutes, mixing vigorously. At this point, the batter has the consistency of thick dough.

6 Meanwhile, finely chop the remaining quartered onion and scallions. Reserve.

7 In a medium-size sauté pan, warm 2 tablespoons of vegetable oil and sauté the chopped onion, scallions, and chile. Add meat, sauté, and then cook for 5–7 minutes. Season with salt and pepper. The meat should be dry. Allow to cool before using.

8 Pour the dough into a bowl and wrap the bowl with a wet kitchen towel.

9 When the dough is cold, knead it with your hands until the dough has the consistency that allows it to be flattened.

10 To make the dumplings, wet your hands and using your palms, make a ball with ⅓ cup dough. Use both hands and flatten it, using your fingers against the palm of your hand to make a circle ½ inch thick. Place 1½ teaspoons of the meat in the center of the circle and close the dumplings, using your fingers to press the edges together. Place the dumplings on a tray and cover with a napkin.

11 Heat the 4 cups of vegetable oil in a frying pan until it is very hot but not smoking.

12 Cover a bowl with a paper towel.

13 Gently place 2 dumplings in the oil at a time. When they are golden, turn them over. Using a slotted spoon, remove them from the frying pan and allow them to drain. Place them on the paper towel to dry. Proceed in the same way with the remaining dumplings. Serve at once.

Pumpkin Soufflé

SERVES 6

1–2 pounds pumpkin, cut in large
  pieces
2 cups water
1 1/4 cups milk
1 small onion, peeled and studded
  with 3 cloves
2 tablespoons butter
3 tablespoons flour
4 teaspoons salt
1/8 teaspoon nutmeg to taste
3 egg yolks, lightly beaten
6 tablespoons fine white
  bread crumbs
6 egg whites
1/3 cup grated Parmesan cheese

1 Preheat the oven to 350 degrees F. Place the pumpkin pieces in a roasting pan with the water and roast the pumpkin for 1 hour. Check the water periodically and add more if needed. Remove the pumpkin from the oven and let it cool for 10 minutes. Remove the skin and place the pulp in a food processor or a blender to make a smooth purée. Reserve and keep warm.

2 Boil the milk with the whole clove-studded onion for 5 minutes. Remove the onion from the pan and let the milk cool.

3 To make the béchamel, melt the butter in a small saucepan, and when it foams, add the flour all at once. Mix together until it forms a big lump. Let it cook as you stir rapidly, making a roux.

4 Pour the milk in slowly as you whisk vigorously to prevent lumps from forming. The whole process should take 5–8 minutes. Season with salt and nutmeg. The béchamel is now smooth and thick. Add the egg yolks and whisk well. Place the béchamel in a large bowl and stir in the pumpkin purée. Reserve.

5 Preheat the oven to 400 degrees F. Place a cookie sheet on the lowest rack of the oven.

6 Coat 6 ramekins or one large 6-cup soufflé mold with butter and sprinkle generously with bread crumbs.

7 Beat the egg whites with a pinch of salt to a stiff peak.

8 Mix 1 cup of the egg whites with the pumpkin purée, folding it in gently with a spatula. Reverse the process and gently fold the pumpkin mixture into the bowl with the remaining egg whites, using circular movements.

9 Gently fill 1/2 of the mold or ramekins with the mix. Place 1/4 tablespoon of cheese in the center and fill the container(s) to the top with the pumpkin mixture. Bake for 8–10 minutes and serve immediately with grated Parmesan cheese.

Collard Greens Mineira Salad

2 bunches collard greens
3 tablespoons olive oil
4 garlic cloves, chopped
1 1/2 tablespoons balsamic vinegar
Salt and pepper to taste
2 cups Manioc Croutons (page 125)
1 yellow bell pepper, grilled,
  seeded, and diced

1 Place a collard green leaf on a flat surface and, using a paring knife, make two parallel lengthwise cuts to remove the core. Proceed in the same way with the remaining leaves.

2 Place 6 leaves on top of one another and roll into a small, tight cylinder (like a cigar). Hold this roll against the cutting board so that just a half inch or so shows. Slice down on this end to make the thinnest cut you can manage (perhaps a sixteenth of an inch). Using a really sharp knife, continue thinly cutting through the rest of the roll. Spread out the now-shredded collard greens over a tray and cover with a damp kitchen towel. Proceed in the same way with the remaining leaves. Reserve.

3 Just before serving, warm the olive oil in a skillet and quickly sauté the garlic. Pour the olive oil over the collard greens and toss gently. In the same pan, warm the balsamic vinegar and pour over the collard greens, tossing again. Sprinkle with salt and pepper. Serve with Manioc Croutons and top with grilled bell pepper.

Salad with Chayote and Pumpkin

SERVES 6

2 chayotes, peeled and pitted
1 pound peeled and seeded
   pumpkin
4 cups water
Juice of 1 orange
8 teaspoons salt
1 tablespoon vegetable oil
1/2 pound filet mignon
1 tablespoon coarse salt
1 1/2 teaspoons balsamic vinegar
3 tablespoons chopped scallions
3 tablespoons olive oil

1 Cut the chayotes in half, lengthwise. Reserve.

2 Cut the pumpkin into 4 pieces lengthwise. Reserve.

3 In a medium-size saucepan, bring water to a boil with salt and blanch one chayote for 4 minutes. Remove chayote from the pan and place in a bowl with ice water. Do the same thing with the remaining chayote.

4 Drain the cold chayotes and reserve.

5 In the same saucepan, cook the pumpkin for 8 minutes. Remove from the pan and place in a bowl with ice water.

6 Using a mandolin, cut the chayote in julienne. (If you don't have a mandolin you can cut the vegetables by using the large side of a grater to cut into slices. Then pile the slices and cut in fine julienne.) Do the same with the pumpkin.

7 Sprinkle the chayote and the pumpkin with orange juice and salt. Set aside.

8 In a heavy skillet, heat the vegetable oil. Pan-sear the meat on all sides, creating a nice crust. The meat should be medium rare. Sprinkle with the coarse salt and vinegar and reserve. When the meat has cooled, cut in fine strips and reserve. In a large bowl, toss the chayote and the pumpkin with the chopped scallions and olive oil.

9 Take a large round plate and make a pile in the center with the vegetables. Distribute the meat around it and garnish with scallions.

Baked Fish, Pirapora-Style

SERVES 6

2 large red bell peppers
1 yellow bell pepper
$^1/_2$ cup vegetable oil
3 medium onions, coarsely chopped
5 garlic cloves, coarsely chopped
$^1/_2$ cup chopped cilantro
1 pound tomatoes, peeled, seeded, and cut in large pieces or 1 (16-ounce) can tomatoes
3 cups fish stock, divided
12 teaspoons salt, divided
4 teaspoons pepper
1 bay leaf
6 (6–8 ounce) fish filets (yellow tail, tilapia, or kingfish)*
6 cups Flake Cornmeal Farofa (page 138)
2 teaspoons olive oil
6 sprigs cilantro for garnish

* Filets of $1^1/_2$ inches thick work best.

1 Preheat the oven to 350 degrees F. Place the bell peppers on a baking sheet and bake for 1 hour; place in a covered pan to cool. When they are cool enough to handle, peel the bell peppers, discard the seeds, and cut them into large squares. Reserve.

2 In a heavy medium-size saucepan, heat the oil and sauté the onions for 3 minutes or until soft. Add the garlic, stirring well, and then add the chopped cilantro. After 2 minutes, add the tomatoes, stirring well. Add the bell peppers and simmer for 15 minutes more. Add 1 cup fish stock, 6 teaspoons salt, pepper, and the bay leaf; cover the pan, simmering gently for 30 minutes.

3 Remove from heat and let it cool. Remove the bay leaf and purée the cooled mixture in a food processor or blender until smooth and uniform. Reserve.

4 Preheat the oven to 325 degrees F.

5 Wash, pat dry, and pound the filets to standardize the thickness. Rub each filet with 1 teaspoon salt on both sides. Spread 2 tablespoons of the vegetable sauce evenly over the top of each filet. Gently top the fish with $^1/_2$ cup of farofa and press with your fingers so the farofa sticks to the sauce. Remove the excess farofa from the sides of the fish and place the filet in a 1-inch-deep baking tray. Repeat with the remaining filets. Pour 2 teaspoons of olive oil on top of the farofa.

6 Pour 2 cups of fish broth on the bottom of the baking tray and bake for 20 minutes.

7 Garnish the filets with sprigs of cilantro.

8 Serve with the vegetable sauce, Flake Cornmeal Farofa, and Glazed Baked Sweet Potatoes (page 138).

Chicken Stew with Okra

CHICKEN
1 whole chicken, cut into 8 pieces
Juice of 1 lime

MARINADE
3 garlic cloves
1 medium-size onion, quartered
1 bunch scallions
1 bunch parsley
3 tablespoons salt
3 tablespoons wine vinegar
1/4 cup water

STEW
1 pound tomatoes, peeled and
   seeded, or 1 (16-ounce) can
   tomatoes
3 tablespoons vegetable oil,
   divided
1 cup chopped onion
2 tablespoons tomato paste
Salt and pepper to taste
3 cups water
1 bouquet garni (3 sprigs parsley
   and scallions, 1 bay leaf)
1 pound okra, cut into 3 parts
1 tablespoon white wine vinegar

MARINATED CHICKEN

1 Wash the chicken and then rub with lime juice.

2 Place the marinade ingredients in a food processor and blend until it becomes a homogeneous liquid. Place the chicken pieces in a plastic bag; pour the marinade over them and tie the bag securely. Marinate for at least 4 hours.

3 Drain the chicken, scraping off the excess marinade.

STEW

4 Cut the tomatoes into large cubes.

5 In a large, heavy-bottom braiser pan, warm 2 tablespoons vegetable oil and pan-sear the chicken pieces, 3 at a time, until they become golden brown on both sides; keep them warm and covered.

6 Allow the pan to cool for 3 minutes. Reheat the pan to medium-high, and sauté the onion, scraping the bottom of the pan. Add the tomatoes and stir with the other ingredients. Add the tomato paste, mixing well; season with salt and pepper. Add the chicken pieces back to the pan; add the water and move the pieces around, making sure all are coated and soaking in the liquid. Add the bouquet garni and lower the heat. Cook slowly for 50 minutes, occasionally checking the amount of liquid.

7 Warm 1 tablespoon oil in a skillet and sauté the okra, shaking the skillet a couple of times. When the okra is light golden, add the vinegar, shaking the pan again.

8 Gently fold the okra into the chicken mixture. Check the seasoning and simmer for 10 minutes. Let rest for 5 minutes before serving. Serve with rice, angú, and hot pepper sauce on the side.

Pork Roast, Vila Rica-Style

SERVES 8

1 red bell pepper
3–4 pounds deboned pork roast
8 teaspoons salt, divided
3 cups orange juice, divided
18 apricots
2 medium carrots, peeled
4$\frac{1}{2}$ teaspoons mustard
7 ounces ham, cut in $\frac{1}{2}$-inch
 slices
$\frac{1}{4}$ cup raisins
$\frac{1}{2}$ cup pitted black olives
3 tablespoons butter
1 tablespoon vegetable oil
2 onions, cut into 8 pieces
4 teaspoons cinnamon

1 Preheat the oven to 375 degrees F. Place the bell pepper on a tray and bake it for 30 minutes, turning it once. Place in a bowl and cover with foil. When the bell pepper has cooled, take the skin off. Open it, seed it, and cut into $\frac{1}{8}$-inch-wide lengthwise strips. Reserve.

2 Trim all visible fat and silver skin from the meat. Butterfly the meat into a rectangular shape. Cover the meat with plastic wrap and pound the meat until it is $\frac{1}{2}$ inch thick. Place on a glass or ceramic plate, sprinkle with 3 teaspoons salt and 1 cup orange juice. Cover and marinate for 2 hours.

3 Open the apricots in half by pressing with your hands to make them flat. Discard pits.

4 Slice the carrots into sticks $\frac{3}{8}$ inch thick and 2$\frac{3}{4}$ inches long. In a small saucepan, blanche carrot sticks in 2 cups boiling water with 5 teaspoons salt for 4 minutes. Remove and place in a bowl of ice water to cool. Drain, pat dry, and reserve.

5 Drain the meat and discard the liquid. Place the meat flat on the counter. Using a spatula, spread mustard over the butterflied pork. Cover it evenly and completely with the ham pieces.

6 Preheat the oven to 325 degrees F.

7 Arrange the apricots, bell pepper strips, raisins, olives, and carrots in parallel rows on top of the ham.

8 Place your hands flat over the rows and press. Carefully roll the meat, pressing down firmly. Tie the meat with a string.

9 In a cast-iron pan, heat the butter and oil and brown the meat on all sides over high heat. (It should take around 5–7 minutes for each side.)

10 Let cool for 10 minutes. Distribute the quartered onions around the meat, pour 2 cups orange juice around the meat, and sprinkle with cinnamon. Bake in the oven for 20 minutes, basting a couple of times.

11 Let cool for 5 minutes. Remove the string and cut into 1-inch-wide serving pieces.

Cow in Muddy Sauce

SERVES 6

MARINADE

3 garlic cloves
1 onion
$1/2$ cup scallions
$1/2$ cup parsley
8 teaspoons salt
6 teaspoons pepper

RIBS

3 pounds beef ribs
2 pounds manioc
$7^1/2$ cups water, divided
3 tomatoes
7 tablespoons vegetable oil, divided
1 tablespoon tomato paste
Salt and pepper to taste
Bouquet garni (3 sprigs of parsley, thyme, and scallion tied together with 1 bay leaf)
2 large onions, julienned
$1/2$ cup cachaça

MARINADE

1 Place all marinade ingredients in a food processor or blender and blend until it becomes a thick paste.

RIBS

2 Cut the ribs into 3 parts. Trim some of the fat and reserve the ribs.

3 Place the ribs in a large bowl and cover them with the marinade. Cover with plastic wrap and marinate for 8–10 hours, turning the ribs a couple of times.

4 Peel the fresh manioc, cut into 3-inch pieces, and soak them in a bowl of cold water.

5 Boil 4 cups water in a small saucepan. Place one tomato at a time in boiling water for 2 minutes. Remove and place in a bowl of ice water. Repeat with remaining tomatoes. Peel the tomatoes, and then seed and dice them. Reserve.

6 Preheat the oven to 325 degrees F.

7 Strain the ribs and scrape off the excess marinade.

8 Warm 4 tablespoons vegetable oil in a Dutch oven and pan-sear the ribs for 8 minutes on each side or until they turn golden. Remove from the pan and place them in a bowl to keep warm. Add tomato paste to the pan and stir, scraping the bottom of the pan to collect the fond left by the ribs.

9 Season pan mixture with salt and pepper, add the tomatoes, and mix again. Return ribs to the pan, add 3 cups water and the bouquet garni, and arrange the manioc pieces.

10 Make sure there is enough liquid to cover everything. Boil for 10 minutes and then simmer on low for 20 more minutes.

11 Place the Dutch oven in the oven and bake for $1^1/2$ hours or until the meat is falling from the bones. Check the amount of water and add more if needed.

12 Just before serving, heat 3 tablepoons oil in a skillet and sauté the onions until soft. Add the cachaça, shaking the skillet a couple of times. Just before serving, add the onions to the pan.

13 Serve at once with hot pepper sauce on the side, with a small glass of frozen cachaça as the beverage.

Beans from Minas

SERVES 6

1¹/₂ cups red beans
2 garlic cloves, crushed, skin on
1 bay leaf
10 teaspoons salt, divided
1 medium red bell pepper
1 medium yellow bell pepper
1¹/₂ teaspoons vegetable oil
3 eggs, beaten
6 tablespoons olive oil, divided
¹/₂ cup finely chopped onion
3 tablespoons peeled and finely
    chopped garlic
1 cup finely chopped parsley
¹/₂ cup roasted manioc flour
4 teaspoons pepper
¹/₂ teaspoon seeded and finely
    chopped hot pepper
¹/₂ cup chopped scallions

1 Pick over the beans, removing stones and any damaged beans. Rinse the beans 2 or 3 times.

2 In a large saucepan, cover the beans with cold water and bring to a boil. Let boil for 10 minutes. Remove from heat, drain the beans and discard the water. Return the beans to the pan and cover with cold water 3 inches above the level of the beans. Add the garlic cloves and bay leaf and simmer gently over medium heat for 30 minutes. Do not allow the beans to high boil but rather cook slowly. Check the level of the water regularly and add more as necessary. Water should always be 1–2 inches above the level of the beans. Gently stir the beans occasionally. Halfway through the cooking, add 4 teaspoons salt to the beans.

3 The cooking time varies according to the quality of the beans, but it should take around 1–2 hours for the beans to be whole and al dente.

4 Drain the beans, reserving 1 cup of the cooking liquid. Let the beans cool, add 2 teaspoons salt, and toss together. Reserve.

5 Meanwhile, cut the bell peppers in half and seed them. Cut in thin strips and then into cubes, matching the size of the cooked beans. You should have about 1¹/₂ cups peppers. Reserve.

6 In a nonstick skillet, heat the vegetable oil and gently pour in the eggs; cook them slowly, shaking the pan at times. When the eggs are cooked (like an omelet), slide them onto a plate and dice them. Reserve.

7 In a large sauté pan, heat 4 tablespoons olive oil and sauté the onion over medium heat until it is soft, then add the garlic and parsley. Stir. Gently fold in the beans to prevent breaking them. Add ¹/₄ cup of the cooking liquid and mix gently. Now add the roasted manioc flour by pouring it from your fingers in a circular motion into the center of the pan; fold in with a spoon. Add the bell peppers to the pan and sauté for 3 minutes, stirring with all the other ingredients. Place the diced eggs and beans in the pan and mix everything with a large spoon. Season with 4 teaspoons salt, pepper, and hot pepper.

8 Serve on a large serving platter. Sprinkle with scallions and 2 tablespoons olive oil.

Flake Cornmeal Farofa

SERVES 6

$1/2$ cup butter or olive oil
1 medium onion, finely chopped
5 garlic cloves, finely chopped
$1/2$ cup finely chopped cilantro, divided
2 teaspoons Tabasco or Malequeta Hot Pepper Sauce (page 100)
Salt and pepper to taste
3 cups flaky cornmeal
1 large red bell pepper
1 yellow bell pepper
1 pound of tomatoes, peeled, seeded, and diced

1 Warm the butter or olive oil in a heavy skillet over medium heat and gently sauté the onion for 3 minutes. Add the garlic and sauté, mixing with the onion. Put in $1/2$ of the cilantro, sauté for 2 more minutes, and season with Tobasco or hot pepper sauce, salt, and pepper. Add the cornmeal through your fingers into the center of the skillet, stirring gently so the cornmeal absorbs the butter as it cooks at the same time. It should take around 5 minutes. If the farofa is a bit dry, add more fat to the flour. Finally, fold in the bell peppers, tomatoes, and remaining cilantro. Serve warm.

Glazed Baked Sweet Potatoes

SERVES 6

4 large sweet potatoes, skin on
6 cups chicken broth
5 tablespoons unsalted butter
Salt and pepper to taste

1 Preheat the oven to 375 degrees F.

2 Wrap each sweet potato loosely in foil but close the foil tightly. Place them directly on the oven rack and bake for 1 hour or until well cooked. When the potatoes have cooled, cut them into $1/2$-inch slices and reserve.

3 Heat the chicken broth in a medium-size saucepan over medium-high heat until reduced by half. Reserve.

4 Place the butter and reduced chicken broth in a large sauté pan with the sweet potato slices and gently glaze them, shaking the pan and coating all slices. (The potato slices will turn light golden.) Season with salt and pepper.

Black Bean Tutu

SERVES 8

BEAN TUTU

1 pound black beans
3 garlic cloves, crushed, skin on
4 tablespoons salt, divided
1 bay leaf
3 tablespoons vegetable oil
$1/2$ cup crushed garlic
$1/2$ cup finely chopped onion
$1^1/2$ cups manioc flour
Pepper to taste

TUTU SAUCE

1 tablespoon vegetable oil
$1^1/2$ cups red onion, julienned
2 tablespoons tomato paste
$1/4$ cup water
2 tablespoons apple cider vinegar
Tabasco to taste
Salt to taste

ASSEMBLY

4 hard-boiled eggs, cut in 8 pieces
Sprigs of parsley for garnish

BEAN TUTU

1 Pick over the beans, removing stones and any damaged beans. Wash the beans two or three times. Cover the beans with cold water in a pot and boil for 10 minutes. Drain the beans, discarding the water. Cover the beans again with water and add the crushed garlic, 2 tablespoons salt, and bay leaf. Simmer, uncovered, for 45 minutes to 1 hour or until beans are soft. During the cooking period, check the level of water. Add more water to the pot as necessary. Occasionally stir the beans gently to check the amount of water. (During the cooking process, the beans should always be covered with water.)

2 Drain the cooked beans and reserve the liquid. Return the beans to the pot and, using a potato masher, firmly press the beans to make a soft purée. Use the liquid as you go along to help the process. (Do not use a blender or food processor.)

3 In a mortar, mix $1/2$ cup crushed garlic with 2 tablespoons salt. In a small skillet, heat the oil and sauté the garlic-salt mixture for 2 minutes; add the chopped onion, stirring rapidly. Add the garlic-onion mixture to the pot with the crushed beans,

mixing well. Lower the heat and pour in the manioc flour through your fingers while stirring vigorously.

4 Add more liquid to the pan to adjust the consistency of the purée. With a spoon, whisk the tutu rapidly. The tutu should have the consistency of a thick but airy purée. Season with salt and pepper.

TUTU SAUCE

5 Heat the oil in a small saucepan. Sauté the onion until wilted. Add the tomato paste, stirring well and cooking for 2 minutes. Add the water, and then stir in the vinegar. Season with Tabasco and salt. Let it simmer gently on low heat for 3 minutes. Remove from heat and reserve.

ASSEMBLY

6 Lay half of the tutu in a serving bowl, spreading evenly with a spatula. Spread half of the onion sauce around it and arrange half of the quartered boiled eggs. Lay the rest of the tutu, making a mound in the center of the bowl. Arrange the rest of the onion sauce and garnish with the remaining quartered boiled eggs and parsley sprigs.

Pineapple, Colonial-Style

SERVES 6

1 large ripe pineapple, peeled
1¹/₂ cups honey
4 tablespoons peeled and diced
  ginger root
4 juniper seeds
4 anise star
3 cinnamon sticks
3 cloves
¹/₂ cup cachaça

1 Cut the pineapple in half lengthwise and core it. Cut into rectangles 2¹/₂ inches long. Reserve.

2 In a cast-iron pan, place the honey and the rest of the ingredients except the cachaça and simmer gently for 10 minutes. Add the cachaça and simmer for 5 minutes. Preheat the oven to 325 degrees F.

3 Remove the pan from the heat and carefully arrange the pieces of the pineapple with its juices evenly inside the pan. Coat the pineapple with the honey mixture and bake for 30 minutes, basting the pineapple a couple of times.

4 To serve, distribute the pineapple on individual plates with some of the sauce around it. Garnish with 1 or 2 of the spices.

5 Serve the pineapple with a shot of cachaça and ¹/₂ stick of cinnamon. Place the glass on the side of the plate.

Corn Crème Brûlée

SERVES 6

7 ears of corn
4 cups milk, divided
Pinch of salt
1¹/₂ cups sugar
3 tablespoons butter
1 tablespoon cinnamon
2 tablespoons brown sugar

1 With a sharp knife, remove the corn or grate the ears. Process in a food processor, adding 2 cups of milk slowly. Remove mixture and strain over a bowl by pushing down on the mass in the strainer. Place the strained residue in a clean kitchen towel and squeeze out any remaining liquid over the bowl. Discard the solids.

2 Place the batter with the sugar and 2 cups milk in a large saucepan and cook slowly over low heat, stirring constantly. Lower the temperature every time the crème rises in the pan. Cook for 30 minutes. Remove from heat and whisk vigorously until it cools. Coat 6 crème brûlée ramekins with butter and fill with the crème. Place the ramekins in the refrigerator for 4 hours. Just before serving, sprinkle with cinnamon and brown sugar and burn with a special torch.

White Egg and Prune Pudding

SERVES 8

1 pound pitted prunes,
  plus 6 reserved for garnish
1¹/₂ cups orange juice
4 strips of orange rind
4¹/₃ cups sugar, divided
5 tablespoons water
8 egg whites
¹/₈ teaspoon cream of tartar or
  baking soda

1 In a saucepan, gently cook the prunes with the orange juice and the orange rinds for 10 minutes. When it has cooled, place in a food processor or a blender to make a purée. Let it cool.

2 Combine 3 cups sugar and the water in a saucepan and cook to a light caramel color. Using a spatula, carefully coat a 5-cup mold entirely with the caramel.

3 Preheat the oven to 325 degrees F.

4 Beat the egg whites with the cream of tartar or baking soda to a stiff peak. Gently fold in 1⅓ cups sugar.

5 With a spatula, gently fold 1 cup of the meringue in the bowl with the prune purée. Reverse the process, and fold the prune purée into the bowl with the rest of the meringue.

Pour the mixture, distributing it evenly in the caramelized mold. Bake in a double bath for 35 minutes.

6 Turn off the oven and remove the double bath pan. Place the mold back in the oven and let it cool inside the oven for 3 hours, keeping the door ajar.

7 Twenty minutes before serving, pass a knife around the edges of the mold. Reverse the pudding onto a serving plate and allow it to slide down. After 20 minutes, carefully lift the mold as the pudding releases itself off the mold.

8 Arrange 6 prunes around the pudding.

9 Serve with crème anglaise or sabayon on the side.

Doce de Leite Parfait with Candied Banana

SERVES 6

3 bananas, ripe and firm
1/2 cup sugar
2 tablespoons water
1 tablespoon butter
2 cups fresh cream
1 teaspoon vanilla
2 cups doce de leite

1 Peel the bananas and cut them into 1-inch-thick slices. Reserve.

2 Place the sugar in a heavy skillet over low heat and let it cook for 5 minutes. Sprinkle the water around the sugar and let it simmer gently until it turns a light caramel color. (Do not stir it at any point during the cooking.) Add the butter and then the bananas. Simmer for 5 minutes, shaking the pan a couple of times. Using a spoon, turn the bananas to coat in the caramel. Turn off the heat and let cool. Reserve.

3 Beat the fresh cream with the vanilla to a firm stage. Keep it cool.

4 Place the doce de leite in a bowl and whisk rapidly for a couple of minutes to make it smoother. Fold in 1/2 of the cream and reserve.

5 To assemble, take 6 glasses and distribute the remaining cream into the glasses. Add the doce de leite on top and then arrange the caramelized bananas around glasses. Sprinkle with the remaining caramel.

The Cooking of the Cerrado

Were one to see the region of Brazil called the Cerrado from a satellite during the rainy season, it would look like a huge green leaf with darker veins throughout. This "leaf" spreads across almost a quarter of Brazil's land mass and is roughly eight times the size of the state of Texas in the United States or the combined area of France, Germany, Spain, Italy, the United Kingdom, and Ireland in Western Europe. Coming closer, one would see that the veins are, in fact, canopies of trees that run along the many indentations in the fields.

Driving along its roads, one would likely be impressed with the fertility of the area and the variety of plants growing everywhere over the land.

One might also notice a curious detail. Every tree in the rolling fields grows many meters apart from every other tree, and each has a gnarled, fairytale shape. That's because for six months of the year, not a drop of rain falls in the Cerrado. If one made this same trip during the dry season, the fields would be a desiccated pale yellow, and the trees would be dry and seemingly lifeless. This incredible seasonal contrast has pro-

duced the unique flora and food products of the Cerrado.

Considered the most extensive savannah in South America, the Cerrado has its core in the central Brazilian Plateau that includes parts of the states of Goiás, Minas Gerais, and Bahía.

What has shaped the Cerrado is, in fact, a conjunction of natural factors, the most important probably being the rainfall. The region receives between forty-two and sixty-three inches (1100 and 1600 mm) of rain per year, all of it concentrated in the six-month period beginning in October and ending in April, when the dry season starts.

Other determinants are the quality of its water-retaining soil and the fact that this soil feeds the enormous water table beneath it. Both factors foster the conditions that have produced the region's unique drought-adapted life.

As in all savannahs, fire is an ancient element in the Cerrado. The fires were first caused by natural elements such as lightning or volcanic activity, and later they were set by humans to clear the land. But rather than succumb to fire, the trees and bushes of the region have adapted over millennia to survive these harsh conditions. Typically the trees look twisted and bent, with branches stemming from trunks at odd, irregular angles.

The bark of these trees is thick and crusty, and this protects the core of the tree until the rain returns. Also, these trees have unusually long taproots, often thirty to fifty feet (10 to 15 meters) deep, that allow them to draw up nutrients and moisture when there is none at the surface. During the rainy season, the leaves return—and they are huge, perhaps to take maximum advantage of the seasonal abundance.

The dominant trait of this woodland savannah is a class of tall grass that gives a pleasant visual sensation of softness, as if a gigantic blanket has fallen gently over the soil. Where this is the case, the area is identified as *cerrado limpo* (clean savannah). Where various types of trees with curled branches and clusters of bushes are prevalent in all directions over the grassland, the area is named *cerrado sujo* (dirty savannah).

As one's eyes get used to those landscapes, long, large, dark green lines are perceived that mark the terrain. These are, in fact, compact luscious green gallery forests. These wooded areas grow along the brooks of the lower parts of valleys or in humid fields where the water table runs closer to the surface. These areas are the magnificent *veredas*, the oases of the Cerrado, unique regional landmarks.

To accentuate even more the oases' appearance, one of the species that grows in these environments is the *buriti*, an elegant palm tree that grows tall and upright, crowned by huge leaves of bright green. The star-shaped leaves form a round canopy, and looking through them at the sky is a delight.

The veredas in the Cerrado have played an invaluable role to natives, to early explorers, and now to cattle and their keepers. Like the oases in the desert, they are places to find water, food, shade, and rest.

Guimarães Rosa, a Brazilian writer and one of the foremost writers in Latin American literature, lived and traveled in the Cerrado for years. It inspired him. He used the Cerrado and its veredas to create an essential background for the characters of his novels. This brilliant writer from Minas Gerais succeeded in using the Cerrado's veredas not only as a setting for his plots but also as a state of mind for the character Riobaldo. As the hero of the novel *Grande Sertão: Veredas*, Riobaldo describes the veredas in detail, with a profound feeling of nostalgia as he celebrates the Cerrado's beauty, points out the region's isolation, and asserts that both can induce one to a certain way of being.

The Cerrado is an exceptionally rich environment. It is home to 930 species of birds and almost 300 mammals. More than 10,000 species of veined plants grow there, and more than 400 of these are tree and shrub species that are unique to the region. The trees and shrubs start to blossom at the beginning of the dry season, revealing wonderful colors and filling the air with pungent aromas. This is followed by the surge of fruits that grow in great abundance throughout the months to come. This circumstance profoundly changes the daily life of the people in the land, who then need to promptly prepare the products in order to make them last. Due to this burst of fruit in the region, people living there have developed various ways of preserving the fruit, either by concocting delicious jams or by preserving the fruit in shiny syrup and making artistic candied fruits.

Today, there is a well-developed industry for producing frozen fruit pulp. The pulp is ready to be used in ice creams, cakes, and desserts, making it possible for people living far from the region to enjoy the delicious tastes.

Araticum, cagaita, baru, gabiroba, pequi, buriti, mangaba, bacupari, and taperebá are the names of some fruits from the Cerrado that, when pronounced together, make you feel like dancing.

If the sound of the words is good, the taste of the food is incomparable and addictive. These foods have been part of the local cuisine for thousands of years, first with the Indians, then later with the explorers, and now with today's residents. In particular, these fruits are as muses to chefs cooking in the best restaurants in the state of Goiás and also in the rest of the country.

The ensemble of fruits, vegetables, and herbs of the Cerrado, combined with the way local Indians and the Portuguese used them, have resulted in a genuine and authentic cuisine.

The various tribes of Indians who lived in the Cerrado produced a legacy of wonderful dishes and ways of treating food still in use today. The most important group is the food made with corn, and it is best represented by the *pamonha,* whose name come from the Tupi language.

Pamonhas are made with fresh grated corn that is poured into a hand-size pocket made from cornhusks. Sometimes meat, cheese, or vegetables are mixed in with the corn. Once filled, these cornhusk packages are beautifully folded and tied with thin strips of cornhusk. Thus formed, the pamonhas are then boiled or baked.

Although pamonhas are found all over Brazil, it is in the Goiás Cerrado where they have almost a cult following. *Pamonharias,* (house of pamonhas) are found everywhere in its towns. Freshly made pamonhas stuffed with a variety of fillings satisfy the most demanding tastes. Street vendors in the busiest streets sell pamonhas to the hurrying passers-by, and the air is filled with the mouthwatering aroma of corn!

As a local peculiarity, homemade pamonhas are prepared by women who, two

Araticum is a typical fruit of the Cerrado, with a tough outer husk to shelter the sweet fruit inside from the wet-to-dry season changes of the region.

or three times a week, deliver the pamonhas to the residences of their lucky customers. Around dinnertime, they come strolling on the streets pulling their carts, stopping at the houses to sell the warm and velvety yellow pamonhas, and sipping coffee and chatting with their clients about the latest of their families' events.

In the seventeenth century, Portuguese and Bandeirantes (organized groups of people from São Paulo and Minas Gerais) arrived in the region in search of gold. Having brought their culinary habits to the region, they left their indelible marks in the cooking of the Cerrado's Goiás.

During their extended travel, the explorers used to eat foods that were easy to obtain and would last for a long time. One of them was cooked meat preserved in animal fat and stored in large tin cans. These are still commonly found today in some homes in the region.

Another very interesting dish made with chicken is called *matula*. First the chicken is deboned, and then the meat is finely ground. Then, bacon, cornmeal, salt, and spices are added. The mixture is wrapped in a dry cornhusk and tied, forming sturdy little packages. The bacon acts as a preservative, allowing the food to last for a long time.

When the travelers stopped after a long journey, horses were tied and unsaddled, a fire was lit, and the matulas were baked on top of the hot coals.

The Portuguese women living in towns such as Old Goiás and Pirenópolis showed a remarkable ability in adapting their traditional recipes to the native fruits and vegetables. The combination of their cultural influences and the exotic regional flora produced some of the most interesting cooking in Brazilian cuisine.

Some of the original dishes from that time have come to be icons of Cerrado cuisine. The most popular are the dishes made with the pequi (also spelled piqui), an intriguing bright yellow fruit with a strong aroma that grows on a large tree with such a generous canopy that one can spot and recognize it from miles away. Among the most popular dishes are pequi rice and pequi chicken stew.

Another traditional dish is the *empadão goiâno*. This medium-size pie is freshly baked in earthenware ceramic molds and is found in all types of eating establishments. The filling includes roast pork, cooked chicken, hard-boiled eggs, cheese, and a fragrant, spicy tomato sauce. Black olives and *guariroba*, a small yellow fruit, add a distinct taste to the filling.

One of the most popular traditional desserts is the *pastelim*, the Cerrado's interpretation of the typical Portuguese pastry known as *pastelinhos de Belém* (Belém tiny pie), which is found in Lisbon. The typical puff pastry is filled with caramelized milk custard perfumed with vanilla and orange zest.

Typical desserts made with eggs in Portugal receive the addition of milk here in Brazil. This is the case of *ambrosia*, a mix of mousse and custard of an incomparable softness that is today the traditional dessert at the house

When I was a child, my family and I used to go to a friend's farm expressly to participate in the pamonhada (making of

the pamonha). The process began at dawn. I recall the aroma of strong coffee, corn bread, and freshly baked cake and the noises of the comings and goings of adults getting everything ready for what looked like a grand moment.

Outside on the large patio, surrounded by beautiful trees, were piles of recently harvested corn, many long benches arranged around the mound of corn, huge baskets, huge deep wood trays, and the large corn graters rustically made with tin and wood. Everybody involved in the process sat on the benches around the pile of corn and then the tasks were divided: some stripped the corn, some carefully removed the corn silk, others grated the ears, and some prepared the husks that gave the final touch to the pamonhas.

And then there was the singing! Someone would start a song whose words made reference to the occasion and the rest of the group would tag along to be followed by another song, and so on. . . .

An employee would pass a basket with fruit, freshly brewed coffee, and a tray with slices of the farm's cheese. The function would last until lunch, when all of us would go inside to eat an appetizing lunch and drink aluá, a drink made with skins of pineapple. I don't remember much about the continuing efforts after that, for it was time for us children to go explore the trails and find trees to climb, fruit to pick, bugs to chase, and brooks to jump in! We only came back when the sun hid behind the mountains, reminding us that it was time to go back to the farmhouse where another party was about to start: the cooking of the pamonhas in a gigantic (at least to me as a child) copper pan over an open fire. The vapors over the boiling water made clouds in the kitchen air.

All of the work and waiting were justified by the magic moment when I was given a cheese pamonha. It almost burned my fingers as I untied it and opened the husk, unveiling the yellow creamy cake with melting cheese in the interior. A couple of seconds later I was gulping down the pamonha, eating it all and finishing by licking what was left in between the husks.

As we left the farm and I looked back through the rear window of my father's car, all I could think was how much time I would have to wait until the next pamonhada . . .

of the governor of the state of Goiás. Today, ingredients from the Cerrado are found in many markets around Brazil.

In fine restaurants in Brasilia, Goiânia, Goiás Velho, Perinópolis, Belo Horizonte, and São Paulo, chefs who have lived or have traveled in the region discover new ways to include these fantastic products in some traditional dishes. Tasty veal "ragout" becomes exquisite with the addition of the cashew from the Cerrado; a pesto made with the nut *baru* becomes original; and cornmeal profiteroles with crème anglaise made with pequi are a surprise.

And the surprise doesn't end here: some products of the Cerrado can be found outside of Brazil in specialty food stores, since companies are starting to export these delights, which undoubtedly will come to be appreciated around the world.

In the picturesque eighteenth-century towns of the Cerrado, the culinary arts go further than just cooking.

Cora Coralina, one of the best-known female poets in Brazil, was also a gifted doceira, a woman who makes sweets. As she worked with her hands making candied fruits from the Cerrado, she let her thoughts drift and she formed new poems. Her poems mirrored the art of making sweets, as she beautifully described the household environment of doceiras, their kitchen, their hands, and the delicate and precise gestures they make. Cora's poetry honors the talent of the candy-makers, immortalizing their work as artists and elevating it to the highest rank. Today, Cora's house is a charming museum where one may wander and still feel her presence.

In one of Cora Coralina's poems, she cites the *alfenim*, a candy of Arabic origin that was brought by the Portuguese. She makes reference to Dona Silvia Curado and her fairy fingers.

I once visited Dona Silvia and marveled as I watched her work. She combined sugar, water, and drops of lime and then boiled the mixture over high heat on a woodstove to the stage of thick syrup. From that point on, she worked fast by pulling the still-hot mixture, using three fingers that were expressly covered with manioc starch to prevent the sugar mixture from sticking and burning her hands. When she "felt" the sugar candy had reached the correct stage, she took a piece of candy the size of a soup spoon and then some small nail scissors with curved blades and magically, moving around the candied sugar, she cut here, moved the piece once more, snipped there, and here again, and so on . . . I began to perceive shapes surfacing: doves, flowers, fish, angels . . . even a rabbit!

the recipes
of the cerrado

Giló Puff Pastry Tart

SERVES 6

FILLING

3 pounds green gilós, cut in 4
    pieces lengthwise
4 tablespoons olive oil
3 tablespoons balsamic vinegar
3 teaspoons salt
3 teaspoons pepper

DOUGH

9 tablespoons chilled unsalted
    butter
1 1/2 cups all purpose flour
Pinch of salt
1/2 cup ice water
3 tablespoons tomato paste
3 1/2 tablespoons olive oil, divided
3 teaspoons sugar

GARNISH

3 cherry tomatoes, cut in half
6 sprigs parsley
Balsamic vinegar

FILLING

1 Preheat the oven to 375 degrees F. Toss the cut gilós with the olive oil. Place the gilós in a roasting pan and bake them for 30 minutes, turning them once or twice. They should be soft but not mushy, golden brown and not too dark.

2 Remove from the oven and, while still hot, toss the gilós with balsamic vinegar, salt, and pepper. Let cool and reserve.

DOUGH

3 Cut the butter into small cubes and place in the freezer for 10 minutes.

In a large bowl, mix the flour with the salt. Place the chilled butter in the bowl and, with the tips of your fingers, press the flour with the butter, forming crumbs. Make a small hole in the center of the bowl and pour 1/4 of the ice water into it. Gently mix the water with the flour and butter mixture by moving your fingers like the wings of a butterfly. The flour will flow through your fingers and it will absorb the water (the result should not be too wet). Proceed in the same way until no dry flour is left on the bottom of the bowl.

4 Place the dough on a cold counter. With the palm of one hand, mash the dough to combine the flour and the butter. Repeat in order to create a marbled texture. Wrap the dough with plastic wrap and refrigerate for 30 minutes.

5 Remove the dough from the refrigerator. Sprinkle flour over a cold counter and start flattening the dough slowly by pressing the rolling pin to make indents. Turn the dough 90 degrees and proceed in the same way until the dough is 1/2 inch thick. Add more flour to the counter as needed. Working rapidly with the rolling pin, flatten the dough, making sure not to press too hard. Turn the dough clockwise 45 degrees each time and proceed in the same way. You should have a large rectangle. Fold in four parts like a book and wrap in plastic wrap again. Refrigerate for 30 minutes.

6 Cover a cookie sheet with parchment paper. Remove dough from the refrigerator and flatten the dough to form a rectangle 8 x 12 x 1/2 inch thick. Using a drinking glass or a 4-inch-diameter cutter, cut circles in the dough. You should get 5–6 circles. Place the circles on the cookie sheet and refrigerate for 15 minutes. (Combine all unused pieces of dough, wrap in plastic wrap, and refrigerate for future use.)

7 Mix the tomato paste and 1 1/2 tablespoons olive oil to form a soft paste. Remove the cookie sheet from the refrigerator and, using a spatula, gently spread the tomato paste around the circles.

8 Preheat oven to 375 degrees F. Place the gilós on top of the tomato paste, forming a decorative pattern. (If the dough looks soft, refrigerate the cookie sheet for 15 minutes. The dough is better when it goes into the oven very cold.)

9 Place the cookie sheet on the lowest rack of the oven and bake for 20 minutes. At this point, you may see some butter running, but it will dry during the baking process.

10 Raise the cookie sheet to the middle rack of the oven and bake for another 10 minutes or until golden. Remove from the oven and brush the gilós with the remaining olive oil. Sprinkle with sugar and salt.

11 Place the pies on individual plates and decorate with the cherry tomatoes, parsley, and drops of balsamic vinegar.

Pamonha (Corn Cakes in Cornhusk Papillote)

YIELDS 10 PAMONHAS

10 ears of corn
2 teaspoons garlic powder
8 teaspoons salt
2 teaspoons pepper
2 tablespoons butter
10 1/2-inch cubes mozzarella
   cheese
Pinch of sugar

1 Using a sharp knife, cut off the bottom of the ear of corn and strip off the husks, keeping the large ones and discarding the rest. Flatten the husks and place a weight on top of them. Remove the corn silk from the ears. Grate the ears of corn over a large bowl. Using a sharp knife, scrape each corncob to get everything that is left.

2 Strain the grated corn and season it with the garlic powder, salt, and pepper. Melt the butter and add to the corn.

3 Make little packets using 2 husks and a third one crosswise to go around them. Using a small cup, fill 2/3 of the packets with the batter, and place 1 cube cheese inside with a pinch of sugar. Fold the top of the packet and tie with a piece of string or a piece of cornhusk.

4 Bring 1/2 gallon of water to boil in a large kettle. Carefully place 4 pamonhas at a time in the water and cook them until the husks turn yellow. Strain the pamonhas and serve them hot with more butter. Pamonhas are served hot. They may be served as an appetizer or as a snack with freshly brewed coffee.

Salad with Caramelized Giló

SERVES 6

SALAD

1 1/2 teaspoons molasses or
   pomegranate syrup (found in
   Middle Eastern food stores)
3 teaspoons water
6 gilós*
2 tablespoons olive oil
1 large pita bread
4 cups baby French lettuce
1 cup watercress

VINAIGRETTE

4 teaspoons salt
2 teaspoons black pepper
2 tablespoons wine vinegar
4 tablespoons olive oil

* You may replace gilós with small
  eggplants.

1 Place the molasses in a small bowl and whisk with the water. Reserve.

2 Cut the gilós in half. Coat with the molasses and reserve. Heat a heavy medium-size skillet and add the olive oil. Place 3 halves of the giló flat and pan-sear for 5 minutes. During this time, do not touch or move the gilós. After 5 minutes, turn them over and pan-sear for 4 more minutes. If the skillet becomes too hot, remove from heat for 2 minutes and then proceed. Reserve and keep the gilós warm.

3 Preheat the oven to 375 degrees F. Cut the pita bread into 8 pieces. Place on a cookie sheet and toast for 5 minutes or until lightly golden. Reserve.

4 **For the vinaigrette:** Mix the salt and pepper in a small bowl. Add 2–3 teaspoons of the molasses left in the skillet to the bowl with the vinegar and the olive oil.

5 In a large bowl, toss the greens with 2/3 of the dressing. Place a few drops of the dressing in the center of the plate and make a mound with the greens. Place 2 giló halves on the side and 2 triangles of the pita bread standing by the side of the greens.

Mariinha's Savory Little Corn Muffins

YIELDS 30

1 cup milk
1 cup water
2/3 cup plus 1 tablespoon
    vegetable oil, divided
1/4 cup finely chopped onion
1/4 cup finely chopped parsley
1/4 cup finely chopped scallions
Pinch of salt
4 cups cornmeal
1 cup flour
1/2 cup polvilho (manioc starch)
4 eggs

1 In a large saucepan, bring milk, water, 2/3 cup oil, onion, parsley, scallions, and salt to a boil. Add the cornmeal and the flour at once and stir well. Place the dough in a shallow bowl, add the manioc starch, and start working the dough. Add 1 egg at a time as you keep kneading the dough. The dough should now be soft. Let it rest for 30 minutes covered with a damp kitchen towel.

2 Preheat the oven to 375 degrees F.

3 Coat your hands with oil. Use 2 dessert spoons to scoop up some dough. Using both hands, make strawberry-size balls. Place them on a cookie sheet covered with parchment paper, leaving 1 inch between them.

4 Bake the muffins for 10 minutes or until they rise. Lower the heat to 300 degrees F and bake them for another 10 minutes.

Salad from the Brazilian Savannah

SERVES 6

SALAD
3 cups water
3 teaspoons salt
1 cinnamon stick
2 cups pumpkin balls (cut with
  melon baller)
3 tablespoons olive oil
2 tablespoons cinnamon
4 cups baby Boston lettuce
1 cup watercress
1/2 cup roasted unsalted cashew
  nuts, crushed in pieces

VINAIGRETTE
2 teaspoons cinnamon
3 tablespoons balsamic vinegar
3 teaspoons salt
5 tablespoons olive oil

SALAD

1 In a medium-size pan, boil water with salt and the cinnamon stick.

2 Cook 1/3 of the pumpkin balls at a time for 3 minutes. Strain and place them in a bowl with ice water. Strain again and allow the balls to dry. Repeat the process with the rest of the pumpkin balls. Heat the olive oil in a medium-size cast-iron pan or a heavy skillet; add the cinnamon and roast the pumpkin, shaking the pan to roast the pumpkin balls on all sides. Remove the pumpkin balls and reserve.

VINAIGRETTE

3 Add the cinnamon to the still-warm skillet used for the pumpkin balls, scraping the fond off the bottom. Add the balsamic vinegar and the salt. Whisk in the olive oil.

4 Toss the leaves with half of the dressing. In another bowl, toss the pumpkin balls with 5 teaspoons of the dressing. On individual plates, place a few drops of the dressing on the center of the plate and make a mound with the green leaves. Place the pumpkin balls around the greens and sprinkle with cashew nuts and a little bit of the dressing.

Chicken from the Cerrado

SERVES 8

1¹/₂ cups water
6 tablespoons bacon, cut in small cubes
6 chicken thighs
1 chicken breast with bone, cut in half
10 teaspoons salt, divided
8 teaspoons pepper
7 tablespoons vegetable oil, divided
1 cup diced onion
1¹/₂ cups cachaça, divided
1 tablespoon tomato paste
Bouquet garni: (1 sprig each parsley and scallion, 1 bay leaf, tied with a string)
2 cups chicken broth
2 cups hearts of palm cut in 1-inch slices
4 tablespoons butter, divided
3 tablespoons flour
1 cup Onion Confit (page 66)

1 Bring water to a boil and blanch the bacon. Strain, keeping the liquid and reserving the bacon. Thoroughly dry the pieces of chicken; spread 1 teaspoon salt and 1 teaspoon pepper over each one and then reserve.

2 In a large saucepan, heat 1 tablespoon oil and sauté the pieces of bacon for 3–4 minutes or until golden. Remove from pan and reserve. Add 1 tablespoon oil and sauté the onion for 1 minute. Remove the onion, add to the bacon, and reserve. In the same pan, heat 4 tablespoons oil and sear the chicken pieces on both sides, three at a time, until slightly golden. Remove from pan and place them in a tray, keeping them warm. If necessary, add more oil to the pan as you pan-sear the chicken.

3 In a small saucepan, heat ¹/₂ cup cachaça. When it is hot, pour over the chicken and carefully flambé at once. Bring the chicken and juices back to the pan and add bacon and onion.

4 Add tomato paste, mixing to coat the chicken pieces well. Add 1 cup cachaça, stirring gently to make sure all the pieces are covered with the liquid. Add the bouquet garni, chicken broth, and the cooking liquid from the bacon and let simmer uncovered on low heat for 1 hour, stirring a couple of times. The meat should be very tender. Let cool and reserve.

5 If you are using fresh hearts of palm, bring water to a boil in a saucepan and blanch the hearts of palm. Remove from the pan and place in a bowl with ice water for 5 minutes. Drain the hearts of palm. Warm 2 tablespoons butter in a skillet and sauté the hearts of palm, shaking the pan constantly for 20 minutes or until the hearts of palm become golden. Set aside. If you are using canned hearts of palm, drain, wash, and drain them again. Sauté them as you would fresh hearts of palm. Set aside.

6 When the chicken is cool enough to handle, remove the chicken pieces from the pan and gently separate the meat from the bones. Discard the bones.

7 Return the deboned chicken to the pan and simmer for 5 minutes. Fold in the sautéd hearts of palm. In a small saucepan, make a roux with 2 tablespoons butter and the flour. Whisk 1¹/₂ cups of the cooking liquid from the pan into the roux and cook it for 2 minutes to make a thick sauce. Stirring gently, add the sauce to the pan and simmer for 5 minutes. Finally, gently fold in the onion confit.

8 Serve with rice and Pequi Béchamel (page 171).

Big Pie, Goiano-Style

SERVES 8

DOUGH

4 cups all-purpose flour
1 cup butter
$1/2$ tablespoon yeast
$1/2$ cup water, room temperature
Pinch of salt

FILLING

1 cup vegetable oil
1 pound boneless chicken breast
Salt and pepper to taste
$1/2$ pound pork loin
1 cup tomato purée
$1/2$ cup tomato paste
$1/4$ cup chopped scallions
$1/4$ cup chopped parsley
1 small chili, crushed
2 teaspoons pepper
2 cups water, divided
1 tablespoon butter
2 tablespoons all-purpose flour
2 hard-boiled eggs, cut in squares
$1^1/2$ cup diced manchego cheese
$1/2$ cup pitted olives
1 cup drained and diced preserved
  hearts of palm
3 egg yolks, lightly beaten

DOUGH

1 In a large bowl, work with your hands to combine all dough ingredients. Add water little by little as you knead the dough. When the dough is smooth and uniform, make a large ball. Cover with a damp kitchen towel and let rest for 1 hour.

FILLING

2 In a large saucepan, heat the oil and fry the chicken on both sides until golden. Sprinkle with salt and pepper. When it is cool enough to handle, cut in tiny cubes and reserve.

3 In the same pan, fry the pork loin on all sides. Lower the heat and let it cook, covered, for 10 minutes.

4 When it is cold enough to handle, cut in small cubes. Reserve.

5 In the same pan in which you cooked the chicken and the pork, add the tomato purée, scraping the bottom of the pan. Add the tomato paste, scallions, parsley, chili, and pepper. Add 1 $1/2$ cups water and mix all the ingredients of the sauce. In a small bowl, combine the flour with $1/2$ cup water. Gently add to the sauce and cook for 5 minutes. Remove from the heat and allow to cool.

6 Preheat the oven to 325 degrees F.

7 Coat 8 muffin tin molds or one 10-inch large mold with butter and sprinkle with flour.

8 Sprinkle flour on a working surface and separate the dough into eighths. With a rolling pin, flatten one piece of dough to $1/2$ inch thick. Cut out a circle at least 1 inch larger than the size of the molds. Save the excess dough. Gently place the circle in the muffin mold. Cut out 7 more circles from the pieces of dough and line the muffin molds.

9 Fill the muffin molds in the following layers: cubed chicken, cubed pork, eggs, cheese, olives, and hearts of palm, ending with a layer of sauce.

10 Combine the dough scraps and flatten. Cut out eight circles that will cover the tops of the muffins. Lay a circle on top of a muffin. With the tips of your fingers, press the dough against the edges of the muffin to create a decorative pattern as you eliminate the excess dough.

11 Brush with the egg yolk glaze and bake on the lower rack of the oven for 20 minutes. Move to the middle of the oven and bake for 10 minutes more or until the top crust is golden.

12 Let cool for 10 minutes and serve with a green salad.

Beef with Pequi Sauce

SERVES 4

$^1/_2$ cup preserved pequi
1 pound London broil
Salt and pepper to taste
2 tablespoons vegetable oil
$^1/_4$ onion, finely julienned
2 garlic cloves, peeled and
  chopped
$2^1/_2$ cups beef broth

1 Drain the pequi and cut in julienne. Set aside. Trim excess fat from the meat and then cut the meat in strips and season with salt and pepper. Reserve.

2 In a skillet, heat the oil. Sauté the onions until wilted. Add the garlic and stir well, cooking for 3 minutes. Add the pequi, sautéing for 4 minutes and stirring a couple of times. Add the meat, mixing with the other ingredients and cooking for 5 minutes. Add the broth and simmer for 5 minutes.

3 Serve with white rice or a green salad.

Collard Green Farofa

SERVES 6

3 tablespoons olive oil
4 tablespoons butter
4 garlic cloves, finely chopped
2 bunches collard greens (cut per
   directions on page 124)
2 cups manioc flour
Salt and pepper to taste

1 In a medium-size skillet, heat the oil and butter over low heat and sauté the garlic. Add the collard greens and stir for 3–5 minutes. When the collard greens wilt and become dark green, pour the manioc flour through your fingers into the skillet as you stir slowly, mixing it with the collard greens. When all the liquids are absorbed by the flour, gently mix with a spatula, moving the flour from one side to the other to roast it for 3–4 minutes.

2 Season with salt and pepper.

3 Serve as a side dish with meat or chicken.

Pequi Béchamel

YIELDS 2 CUPS

2 cups milk
3 whole pequi or 3 tablespoons
   preserved pequi, drained
4 tablespoons butter
1 1/2 teaspoons vegetable oil
4 tablespoons flour
Salt and pepper to taste
1 recipe Pequi Rice (see below)

1 In a medium saucepan, gently boil the milk with the pequi for 8 minutes.

2 Remove the pequi and reserve. Reserve the milk.

3 In a heavy medium-size saucepan, melt the butter with the vegetable oil until it foams. Add the flour at once and stir to form a roux. Slowly pour in the milk and whisk, beating vigorously to prevent lumps. Keep whisking for about 5 minutes. Season with salt and pepper. Turn off the heat. Carefully grate the pequi and fold gently into the mixture. If using preserved pequi, chop them extremely fine and fold into the mixture.

4 Before serving, heat the Pequi Rice and the Pequi Béchamel. Gently fold the béchamel into the rice. You should have the texture of risotto.

Pequi Rice

SERVES 6

5 pequi or 3 tablespoons crème of
   pequi or 1/2 cup finely chopped
   preserved pequi
1/4 cup vegetable oil
1/2 cup chopped onion
2 garlic cloves, crushed
2 cups rice
4 cups hot water
Salt and pepper to taste
1 tablespoon chopped scallions

1 In a saucepan, sauté the pequi with the oil, onion, and garlic for 5 minutes or until the onion and garlic turn light gold. Add the rice and sauté for 3 minutes, stirring well. Add water, salt, and pepper and cook over low heat until the rice is cooked and the water has been absorbed.

2 Remove from heat and sprinkle with chopped scallions.

Chilled Cream of Barú

SERVES 6

1/2 cup barú* or 1/4 cup unsalted
  cashew nuts with 1/4 cup
  unsalted peanuts
2 cups water
1 (16-ounce) can condensed milk
2 cups heavy cream
3 tablespoons fruit jam (raspberry
  or blueberry)

* Barú is a nut from the Cerrado.

1 Toast the barú or the other nut combination in a preheated 375-degree F oven for 15 minutes or until the nuts turn light brown. If using barú nuts, peel them by rubbing them between your hands. Bring water to a boil in a medium-size saucepan and boil the nuts, changing the water 2–3 times (a milk will come out of the nut). Drain.

2 Pulse the barú or other nuts in a blender or food processor, crushing the nuts coarsely. Add the condensed milk and blend for 3 minutes. Stop and add the cream. Beat for another 3 minutes.

3 Pour the batter into a medium-size saucepan and let it cook, stirring constantly until it loosens itself from the bottom of the pan. Pour the batter onto a tray; let cool. Chill in the refrigerator. Serve in wine glasses topped with a dollop of jam.

Guava Paste Soufflé

SERVES 8

SOUFFLÉ

11 ounces guava paste
1/2 cup hot water
3 teaspoons butter, softened
2 tablespoons sugar
8 egg whites
Pinch of salt

CREAM CHEESE SAUCE

1 cup of Requeijão (Brazilian
  cheese found in Latin American
  food markets)
1 cup heavy cream

SOUFFLÉ
1 Mix the guava paste with the hot water until it becomes a soft paste. Set aside.

2 Coat a soufflé mold or 8 ramekins with butter and spread sugar around the mold. Shake out the excess.

3 Place a cookie sheet on the bottom of the oven and preheat the oven to 400 degrees F.

4 Beat the egg whites with a pinch of salt to a stiff peak. Fold half of the egg whites with the guava paste and then reverse and fold the guava paste into the remaining egg whites.

5 Pour the soufflé mixture gently into the soufflé mold and, just before serving, bake for 20 minutes.

6 Serve at once with the cream cheese sauce.

CREAM CHEESE SAUCE
7 In a small saucepan, melt the cheese with the cream, simmering gently (do not allow it to boil). Allow to cool before serving.

Mariinha's Sweet Little Corn Muffins

YIELDS 30

1 cup milk
1 cup water
2/3 cup plus 1 tablespoon
   vegetable oil
1/2 cup sugar
Pinch of salt
1 cup flour
4 cups cornmeal
1/2 cup polvilho (manioc starch)
3 eggs

1 In a medium-size saucepan, bring to a boil the milk, water, 2/3 cup oil, sugar, and salt. Add the flour and cornmeal at once and stir well. Place the dough in a shallow bowl; add the manioc starch and start working the dough. Add 1 egg at a time as you work the dough. When the dough is soft and smooth, let rest for 30 minutes covered with a damp kitchen towel.

2 Preheat the oven to 375 degrees F.

3 Coat your hands with oil. Using 2 dessert spoons, pick up some dough. Use both hands to make a strawberry-size ball. Place them on a cookie sheet spaced 1 inch apart.

4 Bake the muffins for 10 minutes or until they rise. Lower the heat to 300 degrees F and bake another 10 minutes.

5 Serve as profiteroles filled with Crème Anglaise with Pequi (page 202) or with Chilled Cream of Barú (page 172).

Pastelim: Little Pies

YIELDS 10 PIES

1 semi-puff recipe (page 196)
2 cups doce de leite
2 teaspoons orange zest
Cinnamon for garnish

1 Coat 10 2-inch muffin tin molds with butter.

2 Open the puff pastry and cover the muffin tins with it. Press in the center and on the edges, forming a decorative pattern. Prick the bottom of each muffin with a small fork. Place the molds on a cookie sheet and refrigerate for 15 minutes. Whisk the doce de leite with the zest of orange. Set aside.

3 Preheat the oven to 375 degrees F.

4 Bake the pastry for 15 minutes on a lower rack of the oven until they turn light brown. Remove from the oven and cool for 10 minutes. Lower the oven temperature to 275 degrees F.

5 Using a spoon, gently fill the muffin tins with the doce de leite and bake for just 2–3 minutes or until the doce de leite melts a little. Remove the pastelim from the oven and let cool for 5 minutes. Using a paring knife, gently remove the pastelim from the muffin tins. Sprinkle with cinnamon. Serve warm.

The King's Table

Transported to Brazil, the table of the royal family became more exciting with the inclusion of Brazilian ingredients adding to its strong French influence. The classic roast chicken, for example, was stuffed with a farofa made with roasted manioc flour and precious dried fruit from Europe. Other native ingredients included new types of roots and vegetables. The cooks incorporated the ingredients gradually, and the dishes soon became regular mainstays of Brazilian cuisine, producing marvelously fragrant new aromas that wafted from the kitchen to the table.

Combining native fruit with traditional desserts or baked goods made with manioc flour and infusions made with local plants were all greatly appreciated.

Here are some examples of how the local and European ingredients were used together.

Roast Chicken, King-Style, Stuffed with Farofa

SERVES 8

1 whole chicken, 3–4 pounds
6 teaspoons salt
5 teaspoons black pepper
4 cups Dried Fruit Farofa (page 178)
2 cups water
2 large onions, cut into eight pieces
4 tablespoons clarified butter
1 cup dried fruit used in the farofa for garnish
1 bunch parsley or watercress for garnish

1 Preheat the oven to 400 degrees F.

2 Wash the chicken thoroughly inside and out with warm water. Drain the chicken and make sure all the water from the cavity is drained.

3 Place the chicken on a cutting board vertically, breast side up. With one hand on each leg, press firmly upward and then inward: the chicken breast will be higher and rounder. Rub salt and pepper inside the cavity and all over the chicken.

4 With a spoon, fill the cavity with the dried fruit farofa. (Do not overfill it, as the stuffing expands with the heat.)

5 Truss the chicken or simply tie legs together at the ends of the drumsticks.

6 Place the chicken on its back in a roasting pan, pour water all around the bottom of the pan, and scatter the onion pieces around it.

7 Place the roasting pan on the middle rack and bake for 50 minutes. During the baking time, brush the chicken with the clarified butter every 20 minutes. Check the water and add more if it dries out.

8 Lower the heat to 375 degrees F and proceed baking the chicken for 20 minutes, but do not brush with butter anymore. To check if the chicken is done, prick the chicken legs with a fork. The juices should come out clear. If not, carefully make a cut between the thigh and the breast, allow the thigh to open to the side, and return the chicken to the oven for 10–15 more minutes.

9 When the chicken is done, place it on an elegant serving tray and remove the strings.

10 Arrange the farofa in a mound on one side of the tray. Garnish with parsley or watercress and the extra dried fruit.

Filet Mignon, Court-Style

SERVES 6

3–4 pounds filet mignon, trimmed
String to tie the meat (8 times the
   length of the filet)
1 cup pitted prunes
2 cinnamon sticks
2 tablespoons oil, divided
$1/4$ cup clarified butter, divided
Salt and black pepper to taste
2 tablespoons cinnamon, divided
6 onions, quartered
1 cup water
1 tablespoon butter
$1^1/2$ cups Porto wine
Edible flowers for garnish

1 Tie the meat firmly with the string. Pat the meat dry and reserve.

2 In a small pan, simmer the prunes and the cinnamon sticks with enough water to cover for 5 minutes or until they become soft. Set aside.

3 Heat a large cast-iron skillet with $1/2$ the oil and $1/2$ the clarified butter. When it is hot, arrange the filet in the pan and sear for 8–10 minutes. (Do not prick the meat at any time. Use tongs or a large spatula to turn the meat.) If the bottom of the pan becomes dry, add more butter or oil. Turn the meat and sear for another 8–10 minutes. Meanwhile, rub the cooked side of the meat with salt, pepper, and $1/2$ of the cinnamon.

4 Remove the pan from the heat, turn the meat over, and rub this side with salt, pepper, and the rest of the cinnamon. The meat should now have a nice brown crust on both sides.

5 Arrange the quartered onions, the prunes with the cooking liquid, and the cinnamon sticks around the pan. Add the water and cook for 10 minutes on medium to high heat, turning once.

6 The meat is cooked when the meat thermometer reads 175 degrees F. Or, you may take a long wooden spoon and press the handle onto the middle of the roasted meat: if you feel some resistance, the meat is cooked to medium-rare. If the meat feels somewhat soft, the meat is rare. (In any case, do not cut the meat to check, as you will lose its natural juices.) If the meat is not cooked enough, return it to the stove for another 5–8 minutes.

7 Coat the meat with the juices of the pan. Remove from the pan and keep warm. Reduce the heat to low, add the water, and scrape the bottom of the pan to collect all the fond and mix all the ingredients together.

8 Before serving, remove the strings from the meat and place the meat on an attractive serving tray. With a slotted spoon, remove the onions, the prunes, and the cinnamon from the pan and arrange them around the roast. Keep warm. Strain the juices from the pan over a small saucepan, add the Porto wine, and simmer for 5 minutes. Whisk in the butter and simmer for 2 more minutes. Pour it into a serving bowl.

9 Serve the meat with the onions and prunes and the Porto wine sauce.

10 Garnish with edible flowers.

Dried Fruit Farofa

SERVES 6

1¹/₂ cups dried fruit (apricots, figs, pitted prunes)
1 cup hot water
¹/₂ cup butter
2 tablespoons vegetable oil
¹/₄ cup finely chopped onion
1 tablespoon finely chopped garlic
3 cups roasted manioc flour
8 teaspoons salt
4 teaspoons pepper
¹/₂ cup Onion Confit (page 66)
¹/₄ cup chopped scallions

1 Cut each of the dried fruit in 3 pieces and place them in a bowl with hot water. Let soak for 15 minutes. Drain, discard the liquid, and reserve.

2 In a large cast-iron pan or heavy skillet, heat the butter with the oil. Sauté the onion for 3 minutes; add the garlic and sauté for 3 minutes. Add ¹/₂ of the fruit and sauté rapidly, mixing well with the other ingredients.

3 Pour the manioc flour slowly through your fingers into the pan and stir slowly. As the manioc cooks, it will absorb the fat. Add the salt and pepper.

4 Lower the heat and keep moving the flour from one side to another to roast it. It should take around 5–8 minutes. Add the remaining fruit and the onion confit and fold in gently. Remove from heat. Just before serving, sprinkle with chopped scallions.

Mousseline Baroa Potatoes

SERVES 6

2 pounds baroa potatoes*, peeled,
  or 1 pound peeled potatoes with
  1 pound peeled turnips
2 tablespoons salt
1/2 cup butter
1/2 teaspoon nutmeg
1/4 cup coarsely chopped scallions

*The baroa potato is commonly
  used in Brazil. It is around 5
  inches long and 2 inches wide,
  with a thin, shiny skin of sharp
  yellow. It is also known as
  "carrot-potato" for its similarity
  to the carrot.

1 Cut the potatoes in large chunks and place in a kettle. Bring water (just enough to cover the potatoes) and salt to a boil. Cook the potatoes for 20 minutes or until they are cooked. Drain, reserving 2 cups of the cooking liquid.

2 Melt the butter with the nutmeg on low heat and reserve.

3 Place the potatoes in a large bowl and mash them in batches with a masher while they are still hot. Use some of the cooking liquid to ease the process. Add 1/2 of the melted butter with the nutmeg. Using a wooden spoon, beat the purée vigorously.

4 Add the remaining butter and beat the purée 3 more minutes or until the purée is airy. It is important that the potatoes are hot during the process.

5 Arrange the purée in a decorative bowl and cut scallions 1/4 inch wide crosswise with kitchen scissors.

6 You may also make quenelles by using 2 tablespoons: scoop a full tablespoon of the purée and press the other spoon on top of it firmly. Slide the empty spoon under the purée and keep repeating this movement until the quenelle has a well-defined oval shape. Serve with roasted meats.

Grilled Pineapple

SERVES 6

1 medium-size pineapple
2 tablespoons sugar
4 tablespoons butter

1 Peel the pineapple, removing all dark spots and imperfections. Lay the pineapple on a working counter. Cut slices 1/2 inch thick. Drain the slices in a colander for 30 minutes.

2 Place the sugar on a plate. In a heavy skillet, heat the butter. Rub the pineapple lightly with the sugar on both sides and gently place the slice

on the hot skillet. Grill for 5 minutes. Before turning, check to see if the pineapple is golden brown. Turn the pineapple and grill on the other side.

3 Do the same with the other slices. Serve with beef and poultry.

Floating Islands with Guava and Porto Sauce

SERVES 4

GUAVA CRÈME

1½ cups milk plus 2 tablespoons, divided
1 vanilla bean
1 tablespoon cornstarch
1 guava, peeled, or 1 cup commercial guava juice
4 egg yolks
½ cup sugar

GUAVA

1 tablespoon butter
1 ripe guava, peeled, cut in slices
¼ cup water
⅓ cup Porto wine or Grand Marnier

FLOATING ISLANDS

4 egg whites
Pinch of salt
4 tablespoons sugar
1½ cups milk
½ cup Porto wine

GUAVA CRÈME

1 In a medium-size saucepan, bring 1 cup milk to a boil with the vanilla bean for 3 minutes. Remove from heat and reserve. (Remove the vanilla bean which you may then store in a clean glass container filled with sugar.) In a small bowl, dissolve the cornstarch with 2–3 tablespoons milk. Reserve.

2 Blend ½ cup milk with the guava until it becomes smooth. Strain and reserve. This becomes the guava-milk juice.

3 Place the egg yolks in a separate bowl and whisk until foamy and light yellow. Add the sugar and beat again to obtain the consistency of a batter. Reserve.

4 In a saucepan, bring the vanilla milk to a quick boil. Gently pour the egg yolks in a stream and whisk rapidly. Simmer for 3 minutes. Lower the heat, add the dissolved cornstarch to the milk, and whisk well to obtain a homogeneous mixture. Simmer over low heat stirring slowly until it thickens. Do not allow it to come to a boil. Place the pan in a bowl with ice and water to cool. Reserve.

GUAVA

5 Melt the butter in a skillet. Add the guava slices and shake the skillet gently. Add the water and then the Porto to deglaze. Shake the skillet and cook for 2 minutes on low heat. Remove from heat and reserve.

FLOATING ISLANDS

6 Beat the egg whites with a pinch of salt to a stiff peak. Slowly add the sugar and beat a little more. Bring the milk to a boil. Lower the heat. Use two tablespoons, form beaten egg whites into ovals and carefully place 2 at a time into the boiling milk. Let them cook for 2 minutes, turning once. Remove ovals from milk, allow to drain, and place in a bowl.

ASSEMBLY

7 Fold ½ of the guava-milk juice into the cool crème. In large individual wine glasses or decorative bowls, place a couple of guava slices in the bottom. Pour in ½ cup of the cool crème, followed by 2 or 3 of the egg-white floating islands. Pour a stream of the guava-milk juice around it, finishing with the remaining guavas to decorate. Sprinkle with the Porto sauce and refrigerate for 1 hour before serving.

Lemon Grass Tea

SERVES 6

3–5 bunches of lemon grass, cut in large pieces
8 cups water
3 teaspoons honey

1 Wash the lemon grass stalks and bruise them with a sharp knife.

2 In a large saucepan, boil water with the lemon grass for 3–5 minutes uncovered. Lower the heat, cover the pan, and simmer for 10 minutes.

3 Strain the tea in a teapot and discard the lemon grass stalks.

4 Place the honey in a teacup and pour the tea over it. Then pour the tea with honey back and forth into the teapot 2–3 times.

Manioc Starch Flour Cookies

YIELDS AROUND 30 SMALL COOKIES

1 cup sugar

1$^1/_8$ cups butter, cut in large chunks

2 cups polvilho (manioc starch flour)

1 whole egg, lightly beaten

1$^1/_2$ tablespoons lime zest

$^1/_2$ cup all-purpose flour

1 Preheat the oven to 375 degrees F. Cover a cookie sheet with parchment paper.

2 In a medium-size bowl, mix the sugar with the butter, crumbling it with the tips of your fingers. Add the polvilho and begin working the dough with your hands, mixing all the ingredients. Add the egg and keeping working the dough until you notice that the dough is becoming smooth and no longer sticks to your hand. Add the lime zest and mix it in the dough. Cut the dough into four pieces and cover with a clean damp cloth.

3 Place one of the four parts on a counter sprinkled with flour. Use a rolling pin to flatten the dough to 1/2 inch thick.

4 Use cookie cutters in different shapes to cut the dough.

Note: These cookies are better when they are small, such as those served with espresso coffee. Place them on the cookie sheet and bake for 15 minutes or until they turn light gold.

5 When the cookies are cooled, store them in a jar.

The Immigrants' Table

The immigrants brought new crops, food, and dishes to Brazil and have enriched forever the country's already fascinating cuisine. On the other hand, they have also embraced the Brazilian way of eating in their traditional style of cooking. Here are some recipes from the immigrant table accented with Brazilian ingredients.

Esfiha

YIELDS 20

DOUGH

1^1/$_2$ tablespoons yeast
1^1/$_2$ tablespoons sugar
2 cups water, room temperature
1^1/$_2$ teaspoons salt
1 tablespoon vegetable oil
2 cups all-purpose flour
2 cups cornmeal

FILLING

^{1}/$_2$ cup preserved pequi
2 tablespoons vegetable oil
^{1}/$_4$ cup finely chopped onion
2 garlic cloves, finely chopped
6 teaspoons salt
4 teaspoons pepper
^{1}/$_2$ pound ground meat
^{1}/$_2$ cup beef broth
Mint leaves, for garnish

DOUGH

1 Dissolve yeast with sugar and water in a small bowl. Move to a large bowl; add the salt and oil. Add the flour little by little and start mixing the flour with your hands, kneading and pounding the dough. Do this until the dough is smooth and uniform.

2 Make a large ball and cover with a damp kitchen towel. Let rest for 5–8 minutes. Knead again for 5 minutes. Make small balls the size of whole walnuts. Place the cornmeal on a plate and rub the balls in it.

3 Cover the balls with the same towel to prevent them from drying out. Reserve.

FILLING

4 Drain the pequi and dice it. Set aside.

5 In a skillet, heat the oil and sauté the onion until wilted. Add the garlic, salt, and pepper and stir well; cook for 3 minutes. Add the pequi and sauté 4 minutes, stirring a couple of times. Add the meat, mixing with the other ingredients; cook for 3 minutes. Add the broth and simmer for 6–8

minutes or until the meat is cooked. Let cool. The pequi meat is ready to stuff the esfiha.

6 Coat a cookie sheet with oil. Coat a cold working surface with oil and place 1 ball of the dough on it. Press with the tips of your fingers to form a circle of approximately 3^1/$_2$ inches. Press toward the edges to form a higher ridge around the circle. Place 2–3 tablespoons of the pequi filling in the center of the circle, stopping at the ridge. Place on the cookie sheet. Repeat with the remaining dough balls.

7 Let rest for 20 minutes.

8 Preheat the oven to 400 degrees F.

9 Bake for 8 minutes or until the esfiha turns golden. Arrange the esfiha on a decorative plate and garnish with fresh mint leaves. Serve as an appetizer or canapés.

Japanese Okra Robata

SERVES 4

24 pieces okra
4 large shrimp, peeled and
    deveined
4 skewers, 8 inches long
4 tablespoons olive oil
$^1/_2$ cup soy sauce
$^3/_4$ teaspoon wasabi (optional)

1 Wash the okra pieces, brushing each one gently. Pat them dry with a kitchen towel and reserve.

2 Preheat the grill to 375 degrees F.

3 Wash the shrimp and pat dry with a kitchen towel. Keep the shrimp chilled.

4 Place 3 okra pieces halfway down each skewer. Gently fold the shrimp (head to tail making a U) and place on the skewer. Add 3 more okra pieces, distributing all evenly on the skewer. Reserve.

5 When the grill is hot, brush the skewered okra and shrimp with olive oil and grill for 5–8 minutes on each side, brushing again just before you remove them. Sprinkle with soy sauce.

6 In a rectangular flat serving tray, place the skewers crosswise diagonally. Place the soy in a small serving bowl and the wasabi in another. Serve with the robatas and sticky rice.

Linguiça Risotto with Crispy Collard Greens

SERVES 6

4 cups water
1/2 **pound sausage (Portuguese style)**
1 tablespoon plus 3 cups vegetable oil, divided
4 tablespoons olive oil
1/4 cup finely chopped onion
2 garlic cloves
2 cups Arborio rice
6 teaspoons salt, divided
4 teaspoons pepper
2 cups red wine, divided
2 cups finely chopped crispy collard greens (page 124)
6 quail eggs, boiled, peeled, and cut in half

1 Bring water to a boil and blanch the sausage. Remove the sausage from the water, reserving 3 cups of the cooking liquid. In a medium-size skillet over medium heat, pan sear the sausage with 1 tablespoon vegetable oil for 8 minutes each side. Chop the sausage and reserve. Make sure the 3 cups cooking liquid remains heated.

2 In a heavy pan, warm olive oil and sauté the onion for 3 minutes. Add the garlic and sauté. Next add the rice and sauté, stirring well. Add 4 teaspoons salt and the pepper. Pour in 1/2 cup of the heated cooking liquid, stirring constantly. Add more liquid to the pan every time the liquid dries out. Keep repeating this process until the rice is almost cooked. Add the rest of the salt.

3 Add the sausage to the rice and mix well. Pour in 1 cup of the red wine and stir. When it dries, pour in the rest of the wine. The risotto should be al dente. If you find the risotto a bit dry, just before serving add 1 tablespoon of melted butter and 1 tablespoon of heavy cream.

4 Serve topped with crispy collard greens, hard-boiled quail eggs, and freshly ground pepper.

Strudel of Star Fruit and Cashew Nuts

SERVES 6

3 medium-size star fruit, ripe
Juice of $1/2$ lime
4 tablespoons golden raisins
1 tablespoon flour
1 sheet commercial frozen puff
    pastry, 10 x 16 inches (25 cm x
    40 cm)
5 tablespoons good-quality
    fruit liqueur
6 tablespoons crushed toasted
    unsalted cashew nuts
1 egg white, beaten
1 tablespoon butter, melted
4 tablespoons confectioners'
    sugar

1 Cut the star fruit in thin slices and sprinkle with lime juice. Reserve. Mix the raisins with the flour and set aside.

2 Carefully unfold the frozen puff pastry. Place it on a cookie sheet covered with parchment paper. Distribute the star fruit in the center, leaving 6 inches on each side clear. Top with the raisins, the liqueur, and $1/2$ of the cashew nuts. Fold one side of the puff pastry over the fruit, covering it completely. Using a brush or your fingers, spread the egg white along the side of the puff pastry and fold the other edge over it, pressing a little to secure it. Place in the refrigerator to cool before baking.

3 Preheat the oven to 400 degrees F.

4 Brush the strudel with melted butter and place it on the lower rack of the oven for 20 minutes. Move the cookie sheet to the middle rack of the oven and bake for another 10 minutes or until it becomes golden.

5 Remove from the oven and use spatulas to slide it onto a platter. Sprinkle confectioners' sugar over the strudel.

6 Serve at once.

Fruits
of the Land

The recipes that follow include traditional ingredients used in new ways. For a long time, these ingredients have been used in the cooking of ethnic dishes, but in these new recipes, they are the main ingredients.

Little Brazilian Crepes

SERVES 6

CREPES
1 cup all-purpose flour
Pinch of salt
2 whole eggs, lightly beaten
1½ cups milk, divided
2 tablespoons butter
2 tablespoons dendê palm oil
3 cups water
8 scallions
12 teaspoons finely chopped
scallions

FILLING
1 cup Dendê Bechamel (page 99)
½ cup hearts of palm, diced

1 In a medium-size bowl, mix the flour, salt, and eggs with a large spoon.

2 Gradually add ¾ cup milk and whisk, mixing well all the ingredients.

3 In a crepe pan, melt the butter with the dendê palm oil and add to the bowl. Strain the batter and let it rest 10 minutes.

4 In a small saucepan, bring water to a boil. Place cold water with ice in a bowl. Immerse 1 scallion at a time in the boiling water for 1 minute. Use tongs or a large fork to remove the scallion from the pan. Immerse in the ice water for 3 minutes or until it cools completely. With your fingers, press along the scallion to remove the excess water. Place it flat on parchment paper and reserve. Repeat with the remaining scallions.

5 Heat the same crepe pan that you melted the butter and oil in. When it is hot, distribute ½ cup of the batter in the center of the pan as you twist with the other hand to distribute the batter evenly in the pan. Sprinkle 2 teaspoons of the chopped scallions around the crepe.

6 Cook for 45–60 seconds or until the crepe is a light gold. Turn the crepe and cook for another 30 seconds or until cooked.

7 Keep the crepe warm. Repeat the same process until the batter is finished.

8 **For the filling:** Gently warm the dendê béchamel in a medium-size saucepan. Fold in the diced hearts of palm and reserve, keeping it warm.

9 Open 1 crepe and place 3 teaspoons of the filling in the center. Fold the crepe, making a little package, and tie it carefully with the scallion.

Manioc Chips

SERVES 6

2 pounds manioc (not frozen)
8 teaspoons salt, divided
4 cups canola oil
$1/2$ teaspoon cayenne pepper (optional)
$1/2$ teaspoon lime zest (optional)

1 Peel the manioc by removing all the dark coarse skin. Wash it well to remove all dirt. Place in a bowl of cold water and reserve.

2 Using a mandoline or a very sharp knife, cut the manioc in very thin slices and place them in another bowl of cold water.

3 In a large saucepan, bring water and 5 teaspoons salt to a high boil. Blanch the manioc slices for 1 minute and place them immediately in a bowl of ice water.

4 In a heavy, medium-size saucepan, heat the oil until very hot but not smoking.

5 Drain the manioc slices. Place them over a clean kitchen towel and pat them dry completely.

6 Place $1/2$ cup of the dry manioc slices in the hot oil and deep-fry them, turning once. When they are golden, remove from the pan with a slotted spoon and place on a paper towel to dry. Keep them warm. Do the same thing with the remaining manioc. Sprinkle with 3 teaspoons salt. Alternately, you may mix salt, cayenne pepper, and lime zest in a small bowl and sprinkle over the manioc chips.

7 The manioc chips will keep for about a week if stored in a tightly closed jar.

Hearts of Palm
Semi-Puff Pastry Tarts

SERVES 6

DOUGH

9 tablespoons chilled unsalted butter
1 1/2 cups all-purpose flour
Pinch of salt
1/2 cup ice water

FILLING

3 tablespoons tomato paste
2 tablespoons olive oil, divided
3 cups hearts of palm, cut in
  1/2-inch-wide slices, blanched
Salt and pepper, to taste
6 sprigs parsley, for garnish

DOUGH

1 Cut the butter into small cubes and place in the freezer for 10 minutes.

2 In a large bowl, mix the flour with the salt. Place the chilled butter in the bowl and, with the tips of your fingers, press the flour with the butter, forming crumbs. Make a small hole in the center of the bowl and pour 1/4 of the ice water into it. Gently mix the water with the flour and butter mixture by moving your fingers like the wings of a butterfly. The flour will flow through your fingers and it will absorb the water (the result should not be too wet). Proceed in the same way until no dry flour is left on the bottom of the bowl. Place the dough on a cold counter.

3 With the palm of one hand, mash the dough to combine the flour and the butter. Repeat in order to create a marbled texture. Wrap the dough in plastic wrap and place in the refrigerator for 30 minutes.

4 Remove the dough from the refrigerator. Sprinkle flour over a cold counter and start flattening the dough slowly by pressing the rolling pin to make indents. Turn the dough 90 degrees and proceed in the same way until the dough is 1/2 inch thick. Add more flour to the counter and use the rolling pin as needed. Work rapidly with the rolling pin to flatten the dough, making sure not to press too hard. Turn the dough clockwise 45 degrees each time and proceed in the same way. You should have a large rectangle. Fold in four parts like a book and wrap

in plastic wrap again. Place in the refrigerator again for 30 minutes.

5 Cover a cookie sheet with parchment paper. Remove the dough from the refrigerator and proceed to open the dough packet to form a rectangle shape 1/8 inch thick and 8 x 14 inches wide. Press a 4-inch diameter cutter or a drinking glass firmly into the dough to cut circles. With a spatula, place the circles on the cookie sheet and place them back in the refrigerator for 15 minutes. Rather than circles, you may also make a single large pie. (Combine all of the pieces of dough that were not used, wrap them in paper, and refrigerate them for future use.)

FILLING

6 Mix the tomato paste and 1 1/2 tablespoons olive oil to form a soft paste. Using a spatula, gently spread the tomato paste around the circles.

7 Preheat the oven to 375 degrees F. Place the hearts of palm slices on the tomato paste, forming a decorative pattern. Bake on the lower oven rack for 20 minutes. At this point, you may see butter dripping out, but it will dry during the baking process.

8 Lower the heat to 325 degrees F. Raise the cookie sheet to the middle oven rack and bake the tarts for another 10 minutes or until the dough is golden.

9 Remove from oven. Brush tarts with 1/2 tablespoon olive oil and sprinkle with salt and pepper. Garnish with parsley sprigs and serve with a salad of your choice.

Baked Hearts of Palm

SERVES 4

2 whole fresh hearts of palm*
1¹/₂ cups water
¹/₂ cup finely chopped parsley
Parsley sprigs for decoration

VINAIGRETTE
1¹/₂ teaspoon salt
Black pepper to taste
2 tablespoons lime juice
4 tablespoons olive oil

* This recipe works only with fresh
hearts of palm.

1 Preheat the oven to 400 degrees F.

2 Place the thickest part of the hearts of palm on a cutting board. With a sharp knife, cut the hearts of palm in half lengthwise. Wrap the hearts of palm tightly with parchment paper and then with aluminum paper, closing well on both sides. Repeat with the remaining hearts of palm.

3 Arrange the wrapped hearts of palm on a baking tray 3 inches deep; add water and bake for 60 minutes. Check the water regularly as the baking tray should always have water. Lower the heat to 350 degrees F and bake for another 30 minutes or until the hearts of palm are soft and golden on the bottom.

4 Meanwhile, take the thinner part of the hearts of palm and shred it as finely as possible. (It will look like very fine, light pasta.) Reserve and refrigerate.

5 **For the vinaigrette:** Place salt and black pepper in a small bowl. Whisk in the lime juice and then the olive oil. Whisk until it emulsifies.

6 In a medium-size bowl, toss the shredded hearts of palm with 6 teaspoons of the dressing and the chopped parsley.

7 On an individual plate, spread some of the vinaigrette in the center. Place the hearts of palm flat side up. Make 3 to 4 slits and pour a couple of spoonfuls of the vinaigrette on it. Place 3 tablespoons of the shredded hearts of palm on the side. Sprinkle some of the dressing around the plate. Serve at once.

Manioc, French-Fry Style

SERVES 6

2 pounds manioc (you may use frozen)
6 cups water
1 tablespoon salt
4 cups canola oil
Salt to taste

1 If using fresh manioc, peel the manioc by removing all the dark coarse skin. Wash it well to remove all dirt. Place in a bowl of cold water and reserve.

2 If using frozen, defrost first, and then cut the manioc in 3 parts and then in half. With a paring knife, remove the fiber found in the center of the root.

3 Cut the pieces lengthwise in sticks 3 inches long like french fries. In a large saucepan, bring water and salt to a high boil. Blanch the slices for 4–5 minutes and place them immediately in a bowl of ice water.

4 In a heavy, medium-size saucepan, heat the oil until very hot but not smoking.

5 When the oil is hot enough, place ½ cup of the dry manioc sticks in the oil and deep-fry them, turning once. When they are golden, remove from the pan with a slotted spoon and place them on a paper towel to dry. Keep them warm. Do the same thing with the remaining manioc. Sprinkle with salt and serve at once. As an appetizer, serve with an aioli or rouille sauce. You may also serve as a side dish with chicken, beef, or fish.

Caipirinha Mousse

SERVES 8

2 teaspoons unflavored gelatin
Pinch of salt
1/2 cup plus 2 tablespoons cold
   water, divided
4 eggs, separated
Juice, zest, and rind of one lime
1/2 cup sugar
1/2 cup cachaça
2 tablespoons confectioners' sugar
Sprigs of mint for garnish

1 In a small bowl, add the gelatin and a pinch of salt to 1/2 cup cold water and let it sit for 5 minutes for the gelatin to expand.

2 In a medium bowl, whisk the egg yolks until they become creamy. Keep whisking as you add 2 tablespoons water and then the lime juice. Reserve.

3 In a medium-size saucepan, heat the gelatin over low heat and mix it to dissolve. Add the sugar at once, stirring well for 2 minutes. Lower the heat and slowly add the egg yolks as you whisk rapidly for 3 minutes.

4 Remove from heat and add cachaça, mixing gently. Add zest of one lime. Fold in gently. Pour the batter into a bowl and allow to cool for 15 minutes.

5 Place the bowl in the freezer for 20 minutes. The gelatin will congeal at the edges of the bowl.

6 Beat the egg whites to a stiff peak. Lightly beat in the confectioners' sugar.

7 Take the bowl out of the freezer and gently place 1/2 of the egg whites into the bowl. Using a spatula, fold in, making gentle, slow circular movements. Now reverse the process and fold the batter into the egg white bowl, using slow circular movements. The result is a nice light mousse.

8 Take 8 wine glasses and fill 2/3 of each glass with mousse. Place in the refrigerator for 1 hour. Garnish with lime rinds and mint.

Tapioquinha or Beiju

YIELDS 10 LARGE BEIJUS OR
40 SMALL ONES

**3 cups sour manioc starch (polvil-
ho azedo)**
1 cup water or more, divided

1 For a single tapioquinha, place the starch in a small bowl, and sprinkle ¼ cup water over it. It should be wet but not liquid. Using the tips of your fingers, gently rub the wet starch to obtain a loose, granulated texture.

2 Take a small pan (like a crepe pan), 6–8 inches in diameter, and heat over medium-high heat. Place ½ cup of the wet starch in a small strainer. Use one hand to hold the strainer over the crepe pan and the other to press the starch against the strainer. As the flour falls in the pan, use a flat spoon to distribute the flour evenly around the pan. With the heat of the pan, the flour will agglutinate (glue together), becoming a crepe. Flip it over and cook on the other side.

3 To make 2-inch-diameter tapioquinhas, place 3 tablespoons of the starch in the strainer and proceed as above. You can usually make 2 tapioquinhas at a time. Remove from the heat and place them on a tray to cool. They may be stored in jars to be used later as canapés.

4 Fill the mini-tapioquinhas with grated blue cheese mixed with fresh cream, or with mango chutney or any other topping of your preference.

Crème Anglaise with Pequi

YIELDS 2 CUPS

2¼ cups whole milk, divided
**6 strips of preserved pequi or 2
  small pequis**
2 tablespoons cornstarch
3 egg yolks
½ cup sugar

1 In a small saucepan, combine 2 cups milk with the pequi and boil gently for 10 minutes. Discard the pequi and reserve the liquid. Let cool. In a small bowl, mix the cornstarch with ¼ cup milk. Reserve.

2 In a medium-size bowl, whisk the egg yolks until they foam. Add the sugar and beat until it turns a light yellow. Pour in the pequi-scented milk and whisk rapidly. Pour the milk-egg mixture into a clean saucepan and cook at very low heat, stirring constantly with a spoon until it thickens, about 5–7 minutes. Add the cornstarch to the saucepan as you stir. The crème should now be smooth with a velvety texture. To check if it is done, coat a spoon with the crème and run your finger along it. You should have a clean line that doesn't run. Pour the crème into a bowl.

3 To chill, place the bowl of crème anglaise inside a large bowl filled with ice.

Resources

Before looking at the suggestions below, try local markets in your area that provide Mexican and other Latin American products. Or try the Internet to find a local Brazilian supplier.

Useful Web Sites

http://www.amigofoods.com
http://www.brazilchicago.com
http://www.brazilexplore.com
http://www.californiabrazil.com
http://www.CasaBrasilOnline.com
http://www.mercadobrazil.com
http://www.newyorkbrasil.com
http://www.sousawine.com

Food Suppliers in the United States and Canada

Arizona
Fogo e Brasa
4909 E. Chandler Blvd.
Phoenix, AZ 85048
480-783-6060
www.fogoebrasa.com

California
Aliança
197 87th St.
Daly City, CA 94015
650-997-4500

AVP International Market
175 W. 25th Ave.
San Mateo, CA 94403
650-525-0110

Hi Brazil Market
2418-A Artesia Blvd.
Redondo Beach, CA 90278
310-318-2108

Mercado Brasil
1252 Valencia St.
San Francisco, CA 94110
800-994-8446, 415-285-3520

Paraiso Brazilian Imports
6564 Mission Street
Daly City, CA 94014
650-994-9700

Supermercado Brasil
10826 Venice Blvd. Suite 105
Culver City, CA 90232
310-837-4291

Connecticut
Wayside Market
2742 S. Main Street
Waterbury, CT 06706
203-753-2380

Florida
Brazilian Supermarket
3971 N. Federal Hwy
Pompano Beach, FL 33064
954-784-9368

Via Brasil
6620 Collins Avenue
Miami Beach, FL 33141
305-866-7718

Illinois
Casa Brasil
249 Robert Parker Coffin Road Mill Pond—Lower Level
Long Grove, IL 60047
847-793-0013
www.casabrasilonline.com

Supermercado Pepe's
2335 N. Western Avenue
Chicago, IL 60647
773-278-8756

Massachusetts
Allston Café Belo
181 Brighton Avenue
Allston, MA 02134
617-783-4858
www.cafebelo.com

Brazilian Corner Grocery Store
192 Brighton Avenue
Allston, MA 02134
617-787-4407

Café Belo
120 Washington Street
Somerville, MA 02143
617-623-3696

Casa de Carnes
38 Bow Street
Somerville, MA 02143
617-625-1787

Padaria Brasil Bakery
65 Concord Street
Framingham, MA 01702
508-872-8698

GO Latino Market
376 Mystic Avenue
Somerville, MA 02145
617-623-8289

International Market
365 Somerville Avenue
Somerville, MA 02143
617-776-1880

Pao de Acucar Market
57 Union Square
Somerville, MA 02143
617-625-0022

Bibliography

New York

Bradeli Variety Corp.
107 Gramatan Avenue
Mount Vernon, NY 10550
914-667-5447

Brasmar Produtos Brasileiros
212 North Avenue
New Rochelle, NY 10801
914-632-9670

Mineola Deli Grocery, Inc.
269 Willis Avenue
Mineola, NY 11501
516-746-6637

Shop Smart Supermarket
15711 Linden Boulevard
Jamaica, NY 11434
718-659-4370

Trade Fair
3008 30th Avenue
Astoria, NY 11102
718-728-9484

Toronto, Canada

Perola Supermarket
247 Augusta Avenue
Toronto, ON M5T 2L8
416-593-9728

Assunção, Patrícia, et al. *Terra de Minas, Culturas & Sabores.* Belo Horizonte: Prax Editora, 2005.

Bastide, Roger. *Candomblé da Bahia.* São Paulo: Companhia das Letras, 2001.

Bosisio, Arthur, et al. *Culinária Amazônica: O Sabor da Natureza.* Rio de Janeiro: Editora Senac Nacional, 2000.

Carneiro, Edison. *Candomblés da Bahia,* 3rd edition. Rio de Janeiro: Conquista, 1961.

Cascudo, Luis da Câmara. *História da Alimentação do Brasil,* vol. 1 and 2. Belo Horizonte: Editora Itatiaia, 1983.

Fernandes, Caloca. *Viagem Gastronômica Através dp Brasil,* 3rd edition. São Paulo: Editora SENAC, 2002.

Freyre, Gilberto. *Casa Grande & Senzala.* Rio de Janeiro: Editora Record, 1998.

Frieiro, Eduardo. *Feijão, Angu e Couve,* 2nd edition. Belo Horizonte: Editora Itatiaia, 1982.

Gonçalves, Ana Maria. *Um Defeito de Côr.* Rio de Janeiro: Editora Record, 2007.

Gravatá, Carlos Eduardo. *Manual da Cachaça Artisanal.* Belo Horizonte: Editora Belo Horizonte, 2002.

Harris, Jessica B. *A Tasting Brazil: Regional Recipes and Reminiscence.* New York: Macmillan Publishing Company, 1992.

Idone, Christophe. *Brazil, a Cook's Tour.* New York: Clarkson N. Potter, Inc., 1995.

Júnio, Chico. *Roteiros do Sabor Brasileiro.* Rio de Janeiro: CJD Edições e Propaganda Ltda, 2005.

Libânio, Maria Stella. *Fogão de Lenha.* São Paulo: Editora Vozes, 1977.

Silva, Silvestre and Tassara Helena. *Frutas no Brasil.* São Paulo: Ediatare Editora Ltda., 2003.

Index

Metric Conversion Chart

Liquid and Dry Measures			Temperature Conversion Chart	
U.S.	Canadian	Australian	Fahrenheit	Celsius
¼ teaspoon	1 mL	1 ml	250	120
½ teaspoon	2 mL	2 ml	275	140
1 teaspoon	5 mL	5 ml	300	150
1 tablespoon	15 mL	20 ml	325	160
¼ cup	50 mL	60 ml	350	180
⅓ cup	75 mL	80 ml	375	190
½ cup	125 mL	125 ml	400	200
⅔ cup	150 mL	170 ml	425	220
¾ cup	175 mL	190 ml	450	230
1 cup	250 mL	250 ml	475	240
1 quart	1 liter	1 litre	500	260